INDIA

IN ANCIENT TIMES

By Cecilia Jennings

Portions of this book originally appeared in *Ancient India* by Don Nardo.

Published in 2018 by
Lucent Press, an Imprint of Greenhaven Publishing, LLC
353 3rd Avenue
Suite 255
New York, NY 10010

Designer: Seth Hughes
Editor: Siyavush Saidian

Library of Congress Cataloging-in-Publication Data

Names: Jennings, Cecilia, author.
Title: India in ancient times / Cecilia Jennings.
Description: New York : Lucent Press, 2018. | Series: World history |
  Includes bibliographical references and index.
Identifiers: LCCN 2017035780 | ISBN 9781534561823 (library bound book) | ISBN 9781534563087
  (paperback)
Subjects: LCSH: India–History–To 324 B.C. | India–History–324 B.C.-1000 A.D.
Classification: LCC DS451 .J38 2018 | DDC 934–dc23
LC record available at https://lccn.loc.gov/2017035780

CPSIA compliance information: Batch #CW18KL: For further information contact Greenhaven Publishing LLC, New York, New York at 1-844-317-7404.

Please visit our website, www.greenhavenpublishing.com. For a free color catalog of all our high-quality books, call toll free 1-844-317-7404 or fax 1-844-317-7405.

Contents

Foreword

History books are often filled with names and dates—words and numbers for students to memorize for a test and forget once they move on to another class. However, what history books should be filled with are great stories, because the history of our world is filled with great stories. Love, death, violence, heroism, and betrayal are not just themes found in novels and movie scripts. They are often the driving forces behind major historical events.

When told in a compelling way, fact is often far more interesting—and sometimes far more unbelievable—than fiction. World history is filled with more drama than the best television shows, and all of it really happened. As readers discover the incredible truth behind the triumphs and tragedies that have impacted the world since ancient times, they also come to understand that everything is connected. Historical events do not exist in a vacuum. The stories that shaped world history continue to shape the present and will undoubtedly shape the future.

The titles in this series aim to provide readers with a comprehensive understanding of pivotal events in world history. They are written with a focus on providing readers with multiple perspectives to help them develop an appreciation for the complexity of the study of history. There is no set lens through which history must be viewed, and these titles encourage readers to analyze different viewpoints to understand why a historical figure acted the way they did or why a contemporary scholar wrote what they did about a historical event. In this way, readers are able to sharpen their critical-thinking skills and apply those skills in their history classes. Readers are aided in this pursuit by formally documented quotations and annotated bibliographies, which encourage further research and debate.

Many of these quotations come from carefully selected primary sources, including diaries, public records, and contemporary research and writings. These valuable primary sources helps readers hear the voices of those who directly experienced historical events, as well as the voices of biographers and historians who provide a unique perspective on familiar topics. Their voices all help history come alive in a vibrant way.

As students read the titles in this series, they are provided with clear context in the form of maps, timelines, and informative text. These elements give them the basic facts they need to fully appreciate the high drama that is history.

The study of history is difficult at times—not because of all the information that needs to be memorized, but because of the challenging questions it asks us. How could something as horrible as the Holocaust happen? Why would religious leaders use torture during the Inquisition? Why does ISIS have so many followers? The information presented in each title gives readers the tools they need to confront these questions and participate in the debates they inspire.

As we pore over the stories of events and eras that changed the world, we come to understand a simple truth: No one can escape being a part of history. We are not bystanders; we are active participants in the stories that are being created now and will be written about in history books decades and even centuries from now. The titles in this series help readers gain a deeper appreciation for history and a stronger understanding of the connection between the stories of the past and the stories they are part of right now.

SETTING THE SCENE: A TIMELINE

Unified government in India begins to weaken, leading to the rise of the 16 Mahājanapadas; Indian religion begins to resemble early Hinduism.

The Vedic peoples begin to rise to power in India, slowly replacing Harappan government and culture.

Siddhartha Guatama is born and begins to create the new religion of Buddhism; Buddhism spreads throughout the Indian subcontinent.

The great city of Mohenjo-daro is constructed.

The Harappan civilization is established, based around the Indus River.

Magadha emerges as the most powerful of the Mahājanapadas, forming a sizable kingdom; the *Ramayana* is written.

Greek conquests in India create Indo-Greek kingdoms and spread Greek culture across the subcontinent, creating new art forms.

British trading companies gain a foothold in India; the East India Company expands its role in domestic Indian affairs; English colonial rule—the British Raj—begins in India.

Chandragupta is born; the Maurya Empire rises to prominence in India; Alexander the Great conquers portions of India before being turned back; Chandragupta gives up his throne and dies.

The Gupta Empire rules in India, unifying the subcontinent for the first time in centuries.

Led by Mohandas Gandhi, Indians protest British rule, finally winning independence and holding independent elections in 1947.

FACTS AND FIGURES

India is a nation full of diversity. The world's most populous democracy, India is home to around 1.2 billion inhabitants and is the 7th largest country on Earth. In fact, India is so large that is often referred to as the "Indian Subcontinent"—but there is no general consensus on which other countries are included under that name. India's geography is also incredibly varied: more than 4,349 miles (7,000 km) of coastline, plains in the south, deserts in the west, and the towering Himalayas in the north. India's economy is rich in diversity as well—from traditional farming and handicrafts to technological services. There are 22 official languages in India, though Hindi is the most widely spoken.

At the Beginning

India is remarkable from a historical standpoint. First, it nurtured one of the four advanced ancient cultures that modern historians refer to as the cradles of civilization. Each developed along the banks of a major river or rivers—the Tigris and Euphrates in Mesopotamia (what is now Iraq), the Nile in Egypt, the Huang in China, and the Indus in India. The first cities appeared in Mesopotamia in the mid-to-late fourth millennium BC.

The world's first known nation-state was established in Egypt in about 3100 BC, and by 3500 to 2600 BC, the Harappan civilization had begun to rise along the Indus and its tributaries. Some Harappan cities eventually grew to cover more than 1 square mile (2.6 sq km) and supported populations of up to 50,000 people. These city-dwellers lived in thousands of sturdy brick houses lining streets laid out in modern-looking grid patterns. Moreover, recent archaeological evidence from western India suggests that the Harappans carved out an empire larger than those of the Egyptians and Mesopotamians in the same era.

Modern India is deeply indebted to its rich history.

Learning from History

In many ways, modern India is still affected by its most ancient traditions. This is in stark contrast with the civilizations that have arisen from the earliest Mesopotamian and Egyptian cultures. Today's Iraq has very little in common with the Mesopotamian peoples who built the first cities, for example. Indeed, for the most part, the religious, political, and social ideas of the Sumerians and Babylonians who inhabited early Mesopotamia are simply historical concepts.

Later peoples, including Arab Muslims, either conquered and eradicated the earlier customs or absorbed and adapted them.

The same is true in Egypt. The ancient Egyptians worshipped multiple gods and practiced numerous daily customs based on their faith. Over time, many foreign groups—including Persians, Greeks, Arab Muslims, and Turks—invaded or occupied Egypt. This process hastened the disappearance of ancient Egyptian culture. Though modern Egypt honors and respects its history, very

few cultural touchstones from those days remain.

In contrast, a very different situation developed in India. There, many ideas and customs with direct ties to ancient Indian cultures remain partially or even totally intact. A majority of Indians "still worship the same gods," historian SinhaRaja Tammita-Delgoda pointed out. "And they still chant the same verses and hymns, which they recited 4,000 years ago."[1] Another scholar who has written extensively about ancient India, Alain Daniélou, agreed. Because of "the continuity of its civilization," he wrote,

India is itself a sort of history museum, with its separate departments preserving the cultures, races, languages, and religions that have come into contact over its vast territory, without ever mixing together or destroying each other. No invader has ever entirely eliminated the cultures of the more ancient peoples, and new beliefs and knowledge have never [replaced] the beliefs and knowledge of former times.[2]

Though visitors and tourists may have a fixed idea of India, it is in fact a country of incredible and rich cultural diversity. Students and tourists are shown here celebrating Holi, which is the spring festival of colors.

The Original Melting Pot

Despite this extraordinary degree of cultural preservation and continuity, India does not possess a single overwhelming culture. Rather, the country features an amazing amount of cultural diversity and layering. Countless historians and tourists alike have been impressed by the wide variety of different cultures throughout India. It is a country that is home to many different peoples, who have carried down countless traditions and customs through generations.

A number of those groups arrived in medieval and modern times, but some of them date back to India's ancient era. After the passing of Harappan civilization, new religious and social ideas were introduced; later, Persians and Greeks invaded; and later still, a dizzying array of native kingdoms and empires, each with a rich culture, rose and fell. All of these left behind tangible traces of themselves, helping to make India the complex and diverse place it is today.

Gopuras are enormous towers at the entrance of some Hindu temples, particularly in Southern India.

CHAPTER ONE

EARLY EMPIRES

Though the independent Republic of India is less than 100 years old, civilizations have prospered in the Indian subcontinent for thousands of years. From the start, the peculiar geography of the region helped to determine how the earliest inhabitants entered the area and where they initially settled. New arrivals made their home across a vast array of terrains and climates.

Across India's northern border stretches the world's highest mountain range: the snow-capped Himalayas. These peaks, along with those of the Arakan range in the northeast, created a long barrier that kept migrants from central Asia from moving southward into India. Mountains, including the Hindu Kush range, are also found in the northwest. However, several passes that meander through these peaks allowed ancient peoples to enter the subcontinent from a westerly direction.

Those who entered India this way found an enormous plain and river valley stretching southward from the foothills of the northern mountain ranges. Encompassing hundreds of thousands of square miles, this region is dominated by three major rivers—the Indus, the Ganges, and the Brahmaputra—along with their tributaries. It is here that India's first major civilization took root.

Arrival on the Indian Subcontinent

Large portions of the north-central region around the Indus, Ganges, and Brahmaptura Rivers have been lush and fertile at various times in the last few thousand years. So it is not surprising that the earliest humans who entered the subcontinent settled there first.

Over time they, and later arrivals, spread southward, where they encountered another highland region, which consisted of the Vindhyas and Satpura ranges. These mountains, which are considerably smaller than the

Himalayas, lead to a vast southern plateau: the Deccan Plateau (which modern Indians commonly call the South). The Deccan formed during gigantic volcanic eruptions that occurred millions of years ago, long before humans existed. Although the plateau is mostly rugged and arid, it is rimmed by coastal plains that receive considerably more rainfall.

Exactly when early humans first entered India and inhabited the river valleys, the Deccan Plateau, and the coastal plains is unclear. Archaeologists think that the first waves of immigrants came from the west—what is now Afghanistan and Iran—sometime between 400,000 and 200,000 years ago. These people were primitive hunter-gatherers who led a largely nomadic existence as they followed the migrations of animal herds.

No physical remains of these people have yet been found, but evidence of their culture consists of a number of tools they made by fracturing pieces of soft stone to produce flakes having sharp edges. They used these tools to slice through and cut up animal hides. Flaked stone tools of this type have been found in many parts of India, including the Deccan, but they are most numerous in the Punjab, the fertile northwestern region in which several rivers flow into the Indus. The Punjab now straddles the border with Pakistan, which separated from India and became a new country in the 1940s. Most of the Indus River system, which was part of India, is also now in Pakistan.

WRITINGS ON THE WALL

The people of the Indus Valley civilization possessed a form of writing that consisted of about 400 characters, mostly pictograms (drawings or symbols that stand for ideas, objects, or words). The pictograms are most often arranged in small groups of 3 to 10, but never more than 20; these groups may represent individual concepts, words, or expressions. Scholars have so far been unable to decipher the script, which bears no resemblance to any known language.

However, a breakthrough may be on the horizon. A team of scientists based in Chennai, India, has recently built a program that they think will be able to unravel the mystery. The program's algorithm scans images of the pictograms and breaks them up into smaller units—like breaking up a word into its letters. This will help decode the writing in the absence of a bilingual text. Scientists use bilingual texts—that is, the same text written in two different languages—to translate by comparison. The Indus Valley script has no such text, which has been a major obstacle for researchers until now.

Some more permanent settlements began to appear in India between 7000 and 6000 BC, but their remnants are meager, and little is known about those who lived in them. It was not until about 4000 BC that more substantial Neolithic communities arose. An ancient culture is considered Neolithic if it practiced agriculture but continued to use stone tools and weapons. These settlements seem to have started in the northwest—in Baluchistan, now in southwestern Pakistan. The common features of these settlers were stone tools, unique pottery, and a reliance on goats, sheep, and cattle for food.

The Rise of Harappa

Although the exact process is still uncertain, experts believe that these early agricultural communities steadily evolved into India's first major civilization. They call its builders the Harappans, after one of its chief cities, Harappa. Harappan culture is also frequently referred to as the Indus Valley civilization. No one knew that it had existed until 1826 (when India was a British colony). In that year, a British deserter of the East India Company army who changed his name from James Lewis to Charles Masson, first discovered the brick mounds at Harappa. However, he did not realize it was Harappa and instead thought it was where Alexander the Great defeated King Porus in the fourth century BC. About 30 years later in 1853, Alexander Cunningham, an amateur British archaeologist, made his first visit to Harappa,

followed in 1856 by another visit. At that time, the mounds were in good condition, and he discovered some artifacts. However, when Cunningham was to make his third visit in 1872, he discovered bricks were taken from the mounds

Ruins from Harappan cities can tell scientists a lot about what daily life was like—but there are still many unanswered questions.

for a railway. Between Cunningham's second and third visits, British engineers John and William Brunton had searched for track ballast for a new railway near Harappa, on the left bank of the Ravi River in the Punjab. They found masses of fired bricks and used some of them for their railway project.

SPA, POOL, OR TEMPLE?

One of the largest buildings in Mohenjo-daro is what archaeologists think was a public bathhouse. It consisted of a rectangular hall lined with columns. In the center of the hall was a recessed pool similar in many ways to the municipal pools found in many modern towns and cities in the United States. The Harappan version was carefully sealed with a tar-like substance, called bitumen, to make it watertight and featured steps leading downward at each end. There is no doubt that the pool was used, but its exact purpose is still not clear to historians. It is possible that the pool was used for recreation, with ordinary citizens refreshing themselves or relaxing in the water, as in the ancient Roman baths. However, a number of scholars say the Harappan bath may instead have been used for religious purposes. If so, selected individuals immersed themselves as part of some sort of sacred ritual.

Much is unknown about the bath at Mohenjo-daro, shown here.

For a while, the strange discoveries in Harappa were largely forgotten. In 1921, large-scale, systematic digging began there under the direction of India's chief archaeologist, Sir John Marshall. It became clear that the ancient city had been erected in 2500 BC, which meant that India had supported an advanced culture far earlier than anyone had previously suspected. Not long afterward, some of Marshall's assistants discovered an even larger Harappan city at Mohenjo-daro (meaning "Mound of the Dead"), on the right bank of the Indus River, about 400 miles (644 km) south of Harappa. They found that the buildings of Mohenjo-daro also dated to about 2500 BC.

Over the years that followed, hundreds of other Harappan cities, towns, and villages were discovered, and dozens are still being excavated. These sites are scattered over an immense area of around 579,000 square miles (1.5 million sq km). This is larger than all of Pakistan and twice the size of the region controlled by imperial Egypt in the era in which the Harappans reached their height.

Moreover, all the Harappan sites have an extremely similar layout, building materials, and the mysterious script originally found at Harappa. "Our overwhelming impression," wrote two experts on the Indus Valley civilization, "is of … cultural uniformity—both throughout the several centuries during which the Harappan civilization flourished, and over the vast area it occupied."[3]

The natural inclination, therefore, is to see the sprawling collection of Harappan towns as either a large nation-state or an empire. If the latter is true, it was the first empire in Asia and possibly the oldest in the world. The first Mesopotamian Empire—the Akkadian—was not established until about 2300 BC. However, there is scholarly debate about the validity of calling Harappa an empire. Many think that the distant Harappan settlements may have been linked mainly by shared culture but that they may have had their own local rulers, rather than being a unified empire. Scholars have noted that Mohenjo-daro did not serve as an imperial capital or governmental seat of power. As such, it would be inaccurate to claim that the Harappan people were ruled by a single government.

Ancient Urban Planning
Harappans were highly skilled, well organized, and prolific builders. Each of their larger cities was as big as or bigger than the chief Mesopotamian cities of the same era. Harappa, for example, was at least 3 miles (4.8 km) in circumference and supported a population of around 50,000 people. This is extraordinarily large for the time period.

Harappa and the other Indus Valley cities and towns featured a system of urban planning—the grid—that would not be out of place in today's largest metropolises, such as New York. Perhaps the first such neatly planned communities in the world, the roads in these grids are remarkably standardized and uniform. All run either north to south or east to west and converge at almost perfect right angles. In addition, the main boulevards are either twice or one-and-a-half times as wide as the regular streets, and the streets are almost exactly twice as wide as the side-lanes and alleyways.

Lining these roads are thousands of brick houses. Brick was most likely used because stone suitable for building was scarce in that region of India. The bricks were made by pressing wet clay into wooden molds, removing the moist bricks, and either letting them dry in the sun or firing them in kilns. Not only are Harappan bricks the same standard size across the vast Indus Valley, they are remarkably similar to modern bricks. For this reason, the first excavators at Mohenjo-daro initially thought the structures they were unearthing were less than a century old.

The Harappan houses vary in size, most likely according to the wealth of the people who lived in them. Some are small, with only two or three rooms; others are larger, with several rooms clustered around a central courtyard; and still others are clearly mansions, with multiple courtyards and dozens of rooms. Though only sections of the ground floors now remain, many of these houses were originally two or three stories tall. Most had paved floors, a raised brick hearth for cooking, and bathrooms with sophisticated drainage systems. Water ran from peoples' homes out into underground sewage systems. It is among the most complicated and efficient systems in the ancient world.

Very few large, non-domestic buildings have been found in the Harappan ruins, which archaeologists find strange. Harappa and Mohenjo-daro do have large brick citadels, or fortresses, built on the western edges of the city. These may have had defensive or military purposes, but archaeologists remain uncertain. There are also some moderately large structures that seem to have been used to store grain. No large-scale buildings conclusively identified as temples or palaces have been found. One large structure, measuring 230 by 78 feet (70 by 23 m), unearthed at Mohenjo-daro, might have been a palace, but it might just be a mansion belonging to a wealthy family in the community. Scholar John Keay suggested that the lack of monumental Harappan structures may be due to the limitations of available building materials:

Bricks, unlike dressed stone, must be kept small for good firing and are therefore less suitable for towering elevations and long-lasting monuments. Sun, salt, and wind play havoc with a mortar of mud; weight stresses cause bowing and buckling … Even supposing the Harappans had aspired to [copy] the monumental extravagances [large buildings] of their Egyptian contemporaries, it is hard to see how

MONEY ON THE SCALES

Archaeological evidence suggests that the Harappans had a well developed merchant and artisan class, with individual, specialized professions such as traders, potters, brick-makers, smiths, and so on. These workers utilized a standardized system of weights and measures different from the systems used in ancient Mesopotamia, Egypt, and Greece. The basic unit in the Harappan system was a small cube of chert, a flint-like rock. Evidently, merchants and artisans sold their wares by weight, corresponding to multiples of the basic unit. There were two scales of multiples, one small and one large. In the small scale, the multiples were based on doubling (i.e., 1, 2, 4, 8, 16, 32, and 64 units). The larger scale began with 160 units and multiplied the small scale by a factor of 10: 160, 320, 640, and so forth. These standards were common to every Harappan settlement.

Harappans used chert, shown here, to measure value, similar to the money used in modern societies.

they could have achieved them.[4]

With a Little Help from Friends

With a civilization so extensive and culturally advanced, it is unlikely that the people of the Indus Valley could have remained completely isolated from and unknown to the other great civilizations of the time. Indeed, they were far from isolated. The Sumerians and other peoples of Mesopotamia, though situated around 1,300 miles (2,100 km) from the Indus Valley, were well aware of the existence of the Harappans. In fact, the two civilizations carried on a moderately active trade for several centuries.

Some scholars think that the term Meluhha, found in several Mesopotamian documents, may be the Sumerian word for the Harappans.

During the mature phase of the Indus Valley culture, lasting from about 2600 to 1750 BC, small wooden Harappan merchant ships sailed down the Indus and into the Indian Ocean. From there, they made their way northwestward and passed through what is now the Strait of Hormuz into the Persian Gulf. Several Sumerian cities then existed on or near the gulf's northwestern shores. The locals traded their own goods for Harappan grain; semiprecious stones, including lapis lazuli; and cotton cloth. In fact, the

A popular choice for jewelry in the ancient world, lapis lazuli is still a common stone for use in jewelry and other decoration to this day.

Shown here is a lapis lazuli stone set into a necklace.

Harappans were possibly the first people in the world to spin cotton yarn into cloth.

Part of the evidence for this centuries-long trade connection between India and Mesopotamia takes the form of seals, or small disks made of terra-cotta (baked clay). These had pictures of animals, people, gods, or objects carved or stamped into them. Some were pressed into wet clay or liquid wax, leaving an impression that sealed a commercial deal or identified a merchant or other person or his family. It is possible that the Harappans also used seals as a form of currency, though that idea is debated among historians. More than 2,000 Harappan seals have been found, mostly in the Indus region. Several have also been recovered from the ruins of Mesopotamian cities, which indicates that there was trade between the two civilizations.

This long-distance trading network, coupled with the large number of extensive, well built Harappan sites, is very informative. The combination of these factors indicates that the Indus Valley culture long enjoyed considerable wealth, prosperity, and overall success. To maintain a common culture over such great distances would have required a lot of prosperity, for both the richest and poorest members of Harappan society.

The End of an Era
The Harappans' stability and prosperity, along with their commercial links to Mesopotamia, eventually diminished. The main reason seems to be that Harappan civilization went into steady decline beginning about 1750 BC. Historians sometimes refer to the era lasting from 1750 BC to 750 BC as the Late Harappan or Post-Urban period. As the population dwindled and buildings fell into disrepair, fewer and fewer were repaired. Newer structures were smaller and poorly built. Between around 2000 and 1750 BC, the larger Indus Valley settlements had been abandoned, except for a few impoverished squatters who lingered in the ruins for a few generations. Finally, most of the Harappan sites became completely deserted and disappeared from view.

What caused the decline of such a widespread, organized, and successful civilization? Archaeologists and scholars uncovering these cities in the early 1900s asked themselves the same question. At first, some scattered shreds of evidence made some experts suspect that foul play had been involved. For many years, the widespread theory was that the Harappans underwent the same trauma that so many human civilizations have: foreign invaders. Who were these intruders? Where did they come from? Why did they destroy the prosperous and peaceful Harappans? The effort to answer these questions became central to historical studies of India in the 20th century and sparked heated debates that are still ongoing.

CHAPTER TWO

CONQUERING HEROES?

The Harappan civilization may have died out, but life in the region went on. Indian history, like the rest of human history, is a tale of empires that rise and fall as others take their place. After the Harappans came the Vedic peoples, but it would be hard to identify the exact point where one group replaced the other. Instead, it seems likely that one civilization faded into another. Some have defined this transition as a switch from a civilization of cities without language—because Harappan writing has not been translated, but their cities were left intact—to a civilization of language without cities. This is because the Vedic peoples left behind very few archaeological artifacts, such as pottery, but have provided scholars with a rich body of literature.

Colonial Archaeology

Modern scholars call the historical period following the end of the Indus Valley civilization the Vedic Age. Experts differ somewhat on dates for the period, but the most common estimate is about 1500 BC to 500 BC. The term "Vedic" comes from the Vedas, a collection of verses written in an early form of Sanskrit, an Indian language that appeared in the subcontinent sometime in the early second millennium BC. These texts make up the oldest scriptures in Hinduism; the word in Sanskrit means "knowledge," or "wisdom."

For many years, many scholars attributed these verses to a people they called the Aryans. Aryans were thought to be a foreign race swept who into India at the end of the Harappan Empire, initiating the Vedic Age. Not only did these invaders destroy the Harappan cities and towns, the theory proposed, but they also established the basic religious and social ideas and customs on which later Indian cultures were based.

Today, however, the terms "Aryans" and "Aryan civilization" are increasingly seen as both misnomers and outdated. Terms such as "Vedic people" and "Vedic culture" are fast replacing them in history books. New evidence and reinterpretations of old evidence rejected the idea that some lost, light-skinned race conquered the Harappans. Many scholars who specialize in Indian history now refer to it as the "Aryan myth" and argue that the prevalence of this theory reflects more about modern-day archaeology than ancient culture. Scholar Michael Witzel criticized the theory as being little more than "a means of British policy to justify their own intrusion into India and their subsequent colonial rule."[5] In other words, archaeologists working in the era of British colonialism may have wanted to use an ancient invasion of lighter-skinned peoples to prove the validity of their own era's political actions.

Indian archaeologist B.B. Lal described the theory of an Aryan invasion and subsequent extinction of the Harappans as "nothing more than mere myths which, once created, have subconsciously been [encouraged]. Since these have coloured our vision of India's past, the sooner these are cast away the better."[6] Because a few experts still support outdated theories, however, it remains a controversial subject in some scholarly circles.

Origins of the Aryan Myth

Despite increasing resistance to the Aryan invasion theory, it is worth investigating where the idea came from. First, the notion that outsiders invaded India was partly based on a larger theory that became popular in the early 1800s. In the distant past, it claimed, nomadic, warlike, light-skinned peoples migrated in waves from south-central Asia into Europe, Mesopotamia, Iran, and India. At first, scholars referred to these ancient migrants as Indo-Europeans—but the terms Indo-Aryans and Aryans soon gained equal usage. The idea of a large-scale invasion of India also seemed to be supported by the Vedic texts themselves: Sections of these writings describe a war between the powers of light and darkness. Most scholars of the time interpreted this not as a mythic battle between good and evil, but as a real war between dark-skinned peoples and light-skinned invaders.

This light-skinned conquerors theory was highly attractive to the British when they took control of India in the mid-1800s. According to scholarly thought at the time, the white-skinned, advanced Aryans had "created" Indian civilization, but over many centuries, their race had become diluted and degraded by "darker" peoples. In this view, British colonization of India was simply a repeat of ancient history—which, to the Europeans, made it acceptable. British colonizers could view themselves as "neo-Aryans," bringing superior civilization and religion back to India and ushering the region into the modern era.

Attempts to date the supposed Aryan invasion began in the 1850s, when a noted German scholar of

Sanskrit—Friedrich Max Müller—tried to date the Vedas. He suggested they had been written in about 1200 BC. This was only a rough estimate based on the limited evidence he had to work with at the time. As he later admitted, "Whether the Vedic hymns were composed in 1000 or 1500 or 2000 or 3000 BC, no power on earth will ever determine."[7]

Müller and others suggested that the Aryans had entered India in about 1500 BC. This date was highly speculative, as it was based on unsupported ideas about various biblical events rather than real, physical evidence. A devout Christian, Müller thought that Noah's flood had wiped out most of humanity in about 2500 BC. After that disaster, he reasoned, the Aryans required time to develop and multiply as a people and to migrate through Asia; therefore, they could not have reached India before 1500 BC.

These dates, which are completely unscientific, became firmly accepted by the scholarly community in the late 19th century. So, when the Indus Valley

WAR IN FAIR WEATHER

The oldest of the Vedas, the Rigveda, contains numerous hymns to the Vedic deities, including several dedicated to Indra, god of war and rain. This hymn calls upon Indra to help his worshippers achieve victory in battle:

> INDRA, bring wealth that gives delight, the victor's, ever-conquering wealth,
> Most excellent, to be our aid;
> By means of which we may repel our foes in battle hand to hand,
> By thee assisted with the [chariot].
> Aided by thee, the thunder-armed, Indra, may we lift up the bolt,
> And conquer all our foes in fight.
> With thee, O India, for ally with missile-darting heroes, may
> We conquer our embattled foes.
> Mighty is Indra, yea supreme; greatness be his, the Thunderer:
> Wide as the heaven extends his power
> Which aideth those to win them sons, who come as heroes to the fight …
> So also is his excellence, great, vigorous, rich in cattle, like
> A ripe branch to the worshipper.[1]

1. Ralph T.H. Griffith, trans., "Hymn VIII. Indra," Sacred Texts, accessed July 12, 2017. www.sacred-texts.com/hin/rigveda/rv01008.htm.

civilization was discovered in the 1920s, experts immediately tried to fit it into the Aryan historical framework they had already constructed. First, evidence showed that the Harappans had flourished well before 1500 BC. So, experts assumed, they could not be related to the Aryans, who did not arrive until that time. The fact that most of the Harappan cities were abandoned in the early second millennium BC also seemed to fit the Aryan invasion scenario. Simply put, most scholars jumped to the conclusion that the foreign Aryans had overrun what was left of a rapidly declining native culture.

The Vedas, shown here, is an extraordinary text, rich in both religious and historical value.

This idea gained considerable support in the 1940s when British archaeologist Mortimer Wheeler found a fortification wall at Harappa. Because one of the Vedic gods—Indra—is referred to as a deity of war in one of the Vedas, Wheeler saw it as more evidence of the Aryan conquest of the Harappans. He argued that Indra was a symbol of the oncoming Aryan attacks. In short, by the mid-20th century, a majority of scholars accepted the dramatic scenario summarized by Keay:

> The Aryan [nomads] hurtled down the passes from Afghanistan [and onto] the plains of the Punjab. Dealing death and destruction from fleets of horse-drawn chariots, they subdued the indigenous peoples and [stole] their herds. [These natives] were characterized as dark, flat-nosed, uncouth [unsophisticated], incomprehensible and generally inferior. The Aryans, on the other hand, were finer-featured, fairer, taller, favoured above others in the excellence of their gods … and altogether a very superior people.[8]

In other words, if the Aryans really had wiped out the Harappans, it was because they were the superior people, and they deserved victory. British archeologists must have felt that the British colonization of India followed the same path: people who were fair, tall, and altogether superior took land from natives, who the invaders viewed as inferior. The Europeans believed that they had a right to claim these lands. However, that problematic and racist logic—much like British colonial rule in general—would fail to stand the test of time and crumbled under the rigor of truly scientific inquiry.

The Fault in Logic

As time went on, an increasing number of archaeologists and other experts began to suspect that the invasion theory's foundations were shaky. New evidence about the Harappans' demise came to light in the late 20th century. This new evidence proved that although it was true that the Indus Valley culture as a whole declined and eventually died out, pockets of it survived well into the late second millennium BC. In fact, several new Harappan settlements were built during these years in the outer fringes of the Indus Valley. This seemed to indicate a migration away from the central part of the valley. Increasing evidence also indicated that the abandonment of large sectors of that central region had not been caused by violence at all, much less a massive invasion. According to one of Mohenjo-daro's chief excavators during the 1960s,

> There is no destruction level covering the latest period of the city, no sign of extensive burning, no bodies of warriors clad in armour and surrounded by the weapons of war, [and] the citadel, the only fortified part of the city, yielded no evidence of a final defence.[9]

Instead, more and more evidence pointed to major natural, environmental, and economic changes as the main causes of the Harappan civilization's demise. Scholars found that large portions of the central Indus Valley became unusually arid in the early second millennium BC, which must have seriously damaged the farming lifestyle in the region. Agricultural output also declined, Lal pointed out, because of "over-exploitation and consequent wearing out of the landscape." In addition, "a marked fall in trade, both internal as well as external," dealt a huge blow to the Harappans' economy and standard of living. "As a result of all this, there was no longer the affluence that used to characterise this civilization. The cities began to disappear and there was a reversion to a rural scenario."[10] Making all of these factors worse, the Harappans were dealing with a major environmental shift: One of the major rivers in western India, the Saraswati, on whose banks many Harappan towns were built and on whose water the Harappans relied, completely dried up during this period. The Harappans were not wiped out suddenly by foreign invaders; their civilization and culture slowly faded as a result of a changing and challenging environment.

On one hand, this would explain why some Harappans migrated east and west, seeking new land on which to erect new towns. On the other, this new evidence raises an important counterargument to the traditional dating of the Aryans' appearance in India. The Vedas frequently refer to the Saraswati as a wide, flowing river with major Aryan settlements built along its banks. "The Saraswati River went dry at the end of the Indus Valley culture and before the so-called Aryan invasion [in] 1500 BC," David Frawley, an expert on Vedic culture, wrote. "How could the Vedic Aryans know of this river and establish their culture on its banks if it dried up before they arrived?"[11]

The answer is that the Aryans could not have known about and lived beside the Saraswati if they had arrived in 1500 BC, which means they were already in western India at least as early as 2000 BC, and likely considerably earlier.

No matter when the Aryans arrived, the traditional theory claims that they were foreigners with different geographical origins and racial traits. If so, there ought to be measurable differences in physical make-up between them and the indigenous Harappans. To test this argument, detailed scientific studies of hundreds of Harappan skeletons were conducted in the 1980s and 1990s. These found no significant changes in the physical characteristics of peoples living in the region either during or immediately following the decline of the Indus Valley culture. The studies showed that, for the most part, the Harappans closely resembled most modern Indians.

In fact, modern examinations of ancient and modern Indian DNA samples yielded similar results. Some scholars have concluded that if the Aryans were indeed a separate group from outside the country, significant changes should have occurred in the DNA makeup of the inhabitants when the Aryans conquered and replaced the native Harappans—but evidence has not indicated significant genetic or racial differences between the Harappans and modern Indians. Instead, it revealed a remarkable physical continuity among Indians over the centuries. The obvious conclusion seems to be that there was no foreign invasion, and Harappan culture was not overtaken by lighter-skinned conquerors.

Archaeologists tried to categorize the Harappans as being inferior, but evidence has shown them to be excellent planners, merchants, and even gamers. Shown here is an ancient board game from the Harappan civilization.

CHARIOTS

Chariots are mentioned often in the Vedas. For a long time, scholars thought that the Aryans introduced the spoked wheel and chariot—two major innovations in ancient history—to India during their supposed invasion in the mid–second millennium BC. However, more recent evidence shows that the Harappans used spoked wheels well before that time. It is also possible that the Harappans used chariots, an idea they may have borrowed from Mesopotamia or even developed on their own. It is possible that native Indians began using chariots later, as they entered their Vedic phase. Not only is it likely that Harappans could have built and used chariots on their own, but there are other reasons why it is unlikely that an invading army would use them as their transport of choice. One such argument against the notion of Aryan nomads invading with chariots was described by scholar David Frawley:

> *The whole idea of nomads with chariots has been challenged. Chariots are not the vehicles of nomads. Their usage occurred only in ancient urban cultures with much flat land, of which the river plain of north India was the most suitable. Chariots are totally unsuitable for crossing mountains and deserts, as the so-called Aryan invasion [would have] required.*[1]

1. David Frawley, "The Myth of the Aryan Invasion of India," Knowledge of Reality, accessed July 12, 2017. www.sol.com.au/kor/16_01.htm.

Invasion, Immigration, or Imitation?

These and other archaeological and forensic studies and discoveries shifted the consensus among scholars. The new evidence seemed to indicate that no large-scale invasion of Aryans, or any other foreign group, occurred during the Harappan era or in the centuries immediately following it. Rather, it seems that Vedic culture developed out of Harappan civilization, rather than destroying and replacing it. This realization has prompted a number of new theories about India's inhabitants in the third and second millennia BC.

In one of these alternate scenarios, small groups of foreign migrants entered western India a little at a time over the course of many centuries. As they did so, their culture combined with, or was absorbed into, that of the existing Harappans. Eventually, economic, political, and social changes, perhaps stimulated by long-term climatic and ecological problems, brought about the rise of Vedic culture.

Another hypothesis proposes that the Harappans absorbed foreign ideas, rather than foreigners themselves. In this theory, a few outsiders migrated into western India in the early second millennium BC. For reasons unknown, they exerted an unusually strong cultural influence on the existing society. In other words, the late Harappans may have borrowed various religious, social, and technological elements they saw as useful or attractive from influential immigrants. Over time, these borrowed cultural elements brought so much change that the natives developed a new culture, and the Vedic Age began. If this is true, the foreigners left no noticeable traces of themselves in the archaeological and genetic records.

Regardless of whether the Vedic Age emerged as the result of one civilization dying out naturally and a new one gaining prominence or as response to immigrant influence on the existing Harappan culture, Keay argued that "the process appears simply to have been one of gradual [cultural assimilation], requiring neither mass migration nor [conquest]."[12] This theory stresses the continuity of native Indian civilization, a quality observed among the Harappans during their prime and among all the Indian cultures that followed them.

Languages and Cities

Regardless of the exact methods, the Vedic people unquestionably came to inhabit western India. Eventually, this civilization spread into the Ganges River valley and further eastward and southward into the subcontinent. Very little of a concrete nature is known about their everyday lives, habits, and customs. This is mostly because, unlike their Harappan predecessors, they were not highly urbanized; they did not leave behind extensive ruins containing artifacts of daily life for scientists to study. Instead, the Vedic people, at least during the initial centuries of the Vedic Age, were mainly rural and agrarian, raising cattle and sheep and growing a few staple crops. They lived on farms and in small villages, which were impermanent and left few traces in the archaeological record.

Historians may not know exactly how the Vedic people lived, but they do know a great deal about how they thought. Where the Harappans left behind vast cities with only indecipherable language, the Vedic people left behind no cities but volumes of oral tradition, which was eventually converted into literature. Several major literary works survive, describing some of their religious beliefs, myths, and basic political and social structure. The first of these works were the Vedas. The oldest is the Rigveda (meaning "Knowledge of the Verses"), organized into 10 books, each containing many hymns to Vedic gods. The other two most important Vedas were the Samaveda ("Knowledge of the Chants") and the Yajurveda ("Knowledge of the Sacrifice").

Around 900 to 700 BC, religious leaders began to write the Brahmanas and the Upanishads, which supplemented the Vedic texts. Specifically, the Brahmanas explained the rituals described in the Vedas, and the Upanishads were philosophical commentaries that discussed and interpreted the spiritual elements of the Vedic texts. Vedic culture also produced India's two great epic poems: the *Ramayana* and the *Mahabharata*. The *Ramayana* tells of the heroic deeds of Rama, a prince who is also an incarnation of the god Vishnu. The *Mahabharata*, a huge work of nearly 100,000 verses, describes the struggle for a kingly throne within the larger context of divine will and universal fate.

All of these writings were first preserved strictly through oral tradition—memorization and frequent reciting by priests or special performers. Only later were they written down. The two epics, for example, did not appear in book form until about 400 or 300 BC, after the end of the Vedic Age. The first written versions of the Vedas most likely did not exist until considerably later.

The Ramayana *is filled with adventure, heroism, and twists of fate. Shown here is an illustration of part of that epic poem.*

A Constantly Evolving Culture

What these and other writings reveal is that the Vedic people, divided into various tribes, eventually developed small kingdoms, each inhabited by members of a specific tribe. The ruler of each kingdom was called a raja. Much like rulers today, rajas kept a council of elders to advise them on political and social policy. In addition, a high priest guided him in religious matters, and a military expert, probably the kingdom's chief army officer, helped set and enact military policy.

As the Vedic Indian society came to be divided into four social classes (called *varnas* or castes), Indra, the god of war and rain, faded from prominence. Though he remained in the Hindu pantheon (group of gods), his status was now lower than that of some other deities.

Though advanced metal tools dated to around 2200 BC have been discovered, there is a little evidence that iron spread across the entire subcontinent for several centuries. Stone, copper, and bronze became outdated as soon as smiths figured out how to effectively utilize iron. In addition, raising cattle and other livestock, which was the economic mainstay of early Vedic society, became less important than growing crops. In time, the many scattered Vedic tribal states steadily grouped up into fewer, larger, and stronger kingdoms. With the emergence of these kingdoms and the increasing rivalry between them, India entered a new age. The land would soon witness a series of momentous events, among them attacks by foreign invaders and the rise of India's first true empires.

CHAPTER THREE

EAST MEETS WEST

Scholars have largely debunked the theory of an early Aryan invasion that ushered in the Vedic Age, but it is undeniable that in its early history, India underwent a series of upheavals related to invasion. As ancient India built up its kingdoms and became more urban and more politically centralized, it drew the attention of other empires. Persia and Greece were the first invaders, but they would not be the last. India was entering a new age, and it would be made of iron.

Iron and Urbanization

Modern scholars refer to the last centuries of the Vedic Age (around 800 BC to 500 BC) in various ways, depending on the context. Before the 2010s, this era was called India's Iron Age because historians believed this time period witnessed the spread of iron tools and weapons throughout the subcontinent. However, new archaeological discoveries in 2015

have dated iron tools back to 2200 BC. Moreover, scholars looking through the lens of cultural and artistic innovations refer to the late Vedic period as the Painted Grey Ware culture in reference to the widespread form of pottery in India in those centuries.

Another way of looking at the late Vedic Age is as India's second period of urbanization. The first city-builders in the region, of course, had been the Harappans. Their descendants, the early Vedic people, had adopted a more rural, agricultural lifestyle. As city-states and small kingdoms began to appear in northern India's river valleys during the Iron Age, some villages grew into towns, and a few of the towns grew into small cities.

At the same time, local city-states and kingdoms began to grow larger, often absorbing some of their neighbors. For example, Magadha, a kingdom in northeastern India, expanded in size and prominence by conquering some nearby independent states. By about 700 BC, near the end of the Vedic Age, all of northern India and parts of the south were governed by 16 kingdoms. Historians generally refer to them collectively as the Mahājanapadas, typically translated as "great kingdoms" or "great countries." From this group, Magadha emerged as the strongest and most influential kingdom.

These trends of urbanization and political centralization were among the factors that brought the Vedic Age to a close. In its place, a new era rose, and it was characterized by imperialism. A major factor in this shift was the influence of foreign empires, whose interest in India would cause great upheaval throughout the region. In the sixth century BC, parts of the Indus Valley were invaded by the Persian Empire, which was centered in modern-day Iran. The invasion, largely successful, absorbed this sector of India and converted it into a Persian imperial province.

Only two centuries later, a Macedonian Greek king, Alexander III (later called "the Great"), conquered Persia. His military adventures led him into India, where he significantly altered the existing balance of power. Moreover, though he died soon afterward, Alexander left behind Greek governors, troops, merchants, and artisans. They and their descendants subsequently produced a hybrid Greco-Indian culture in the region that had a significant impact on Indian culture.

King of the Mahājanapadas

Magadha, the most prominent kingdom of the age, managed to avoid much of the upheaval that Persia and Greece brought to the Indus valley. This was largely because Magadha was located in eastern India and had no direct contact with the intruders. In fact, politically and militarily speaking, Magadha actually benefited from the invasions. While the western Indian states fell and made huge concessions to the Persians and Greeks, Magadha remained strong and prosperous.

A lack of reliable historical evidence has kept Magadha's history before 600 BC relatively unknown. However, scholars are reasonably certain that by the early 540s BC the kingdom controlled most of the Ganges River valley and was both the wealthiest and strongest of the Mahājanapadas.

Moreover, Magadhan rulers proved themselves to be ambitious. Sometime in the late 500s BC, King Bimbisara (whose reign stretched from around 543 to 491 BC) conquered the kingdoms of Anga and Kosala. Bimbisara's son, King Ajatashatru was no less ambitious than his father. Chief among Ajatashatru's achievements was the construction of a splendid new city—which would later become the capital—carrying on the urbanization trend that began in late Vedic times. Ajatashatru's son, Udayin, took the royal title from the old Magadhan capital of Rajagrha, situated about 80 miles (129 km) south of the Ganges, and gave it to his father's new city of Pataliputra, on the river's northern bank.

It may have been during either Bimbisara's or Ajatashatru's reign that a new religion, Buddhism, emerged in the Ganges Valley. It coexisted with—but did not replace—Hinduism, mainly because its philosophical concepts were compatible with many Hindu beliefs. Buddhism spread rapidly through the rest of the subcontinent and later spread worldwide, becoming one of India's most important cultural exports.

Buddhism spread rapidly through India during Bimbisara's or Ajatashatru's reign. It later spread worldwide, becoming an important influence in the lives of many.

Princes of Persia

While these events were transpiring in eastern India, parts of western India were undergoing political upheaval and cultural readjustment as the result of an invasion from nearby Persia. The Persian Empire had arisen suddenly in the mid-500s BC when Cyrus II, a local Iranian prince, led a successful rebellion against the Medes, who then controlled most of Iran and Mesopotamia. Having taken charge of the lands within the Median realm, Cyrus initiated major military reforms and assembled a large army. Over the course of the next few years, he invaded and annexed foreign lands both west and east of his Iranian-Mesopotamian power base. Among the regions he overtook were Bactria (the ancient name for what is now northern Afghanistan) and parts of the Indian kingdom of Gandhara, in the northwestern Punjab Plain.

A second, larger Persian invasion of India occurred during the reign of the third Persian king, Darius I, who came to power circa 522 BC. According to the fifth-century BC Greek historian Herodotus, Darius first ordered scouts to explore sections of the Indus Valley. These explorers managed to reach the river's delta, and after a journey of more than two years, they returned to Persia with reports of what they had seen.

Darius then launched his campaign. Very little is known about the invasion itself, including exactly when it occurred and the amount of Indian territory seized. Herodotus only described the broad details of the conquest, which ended in a Persian victory. The best estimate of modern scholars is that this Persian invasion began sometime around 515 BC. Though scholars disagree on the extent of Darius's conquest, it is safe to conclude that it included most of the Punjab Plain lying west of the Indus. There is no firm evidence that the Persians ever controlled any Indian territory east of that river.

Whichever Indian lands did fall to the Persians, they became a satrapy, or province, of the Persian Empire. Herodotus mentions this province—called Gandhara, named after the conquered Indian kingdom—as do other ancient historians. He wrote that it was the richest of Persia's many satrapies, supplying the king with gold and other valuables. Indian men who lived in the province also were expected to serve in the Persian army; some of these Indian troops would go on to accompany Darius's son Xerxes on his famous military expedition to Greece in 480 BC.

Greece's Greatest Alexander

The Persians introduced a number of political ideas, religious customs, and Near Eastern languages into western India. However, Persian influences in this region were mostly short-lived, ultimately doomed to be overshadowed by the Greeks. This was partly because the Greek invasion of the subcontinent was more extensive and affected a larger number of western Indian kingdoms.

Alexander the Great's legend often aided his conquests, as cities—or even whole kingdoms—elected not to put up a fight. He is shown here fighting in a sea battle.

Alexander the Great's legend preceded him in these kingdoms. Their rajas had heard of Alexander's extraordinary military skills and exploits well before his arrival; they knew that he had brought mighty Persia, the largest empire in world history up to that time, to its knees. He had crossed into Asia in 334 BC and conquered the Persian territories of Anatolia (what is now Turkey), Syria, Palestine, Egypt, Mesopotamia, and Iran with amazing speed. He then moved eastward into Bactria. By 327 BC, he was ready to push onward into the Indus Valley.

Hearing these reports, Indian leaders were anxious. Few believed they could resist where so many others had fallen. As John Keay explained, many kingdoms simply decided it would be wiser to surrender to Alexander than to fight him:

> Like a tidal wave, news of Alexander's prowess had swept ahead of him, flattening resistance and sucking him forward. Indian defectors from the [Persian] forces primed his interest and paved the way; local [Indian rulers] promised support and ... sought his friendship.[13]

Having met little resistance, in the spring of 326 BC, Alexander crossed the Indus and arrived at the city of Taxila. There, he received a warm welcome from the local Indians. He also received presents and offers of alliance from ambassadors representing nearby Indian states.

Two Great Generals

One Indian ruler was not so quick to surrender to the invaders, however. He was Porus (or Puru), raja of the kingdom of Paurava, located east of the Hydaspes River in the Punjab. Hydaspes is the Greek name for the river; the ancient Indians called it the Vitasta, and today it is known by its Muslim name, the Jhelum. Porus must have been a powerful ruler of a populous realm, for he was able to amass an army of between 20,000 and 30,000 infantry (foot soldiers), around 3,000 cavalry (horsemen), and roughly 200 war elephants along the Hydaspes's eastern bank.

The Macedonians and other Greeks, reinforced by thousands of Indian troops from other kingdoms, marched to the river. As Alexander's chief ancient biographer, the Greek Arrian, wrote that the two armies could see each other across the river. A contest then ensued, in which the Greeks tried to cross the river and Porus attempted to stop them:

> Porus remained on guard in person, and sent [soldiers], each under command of an officer, to the various other points along the river where a crossing was [possible]; for he was determined to stop Alexander from getting over. Alexander's answer was continued movement of his troops to keep Porus guessing. He split his force into a number of detachments, moving some of them under his own command ... others under the command of various officers with instructions to keep constantly on the move.[14]

Porus ordered his troops to follow these mobile units of Greeks closely, in case one of them suddenly attempted to cross the river. Despite these efforts, Alexander managed to find an unguarded spot along the riverbank several miles upstream from his main camp. There, he led a contingent of his army across the Hydaspes. Hearing of this, Porus hurried to halt the enemy advance.

Even before the opposing armies clashed, Porus's forces were already at a disadvantage. Following a clever plan Alexander had devised, one of his generals, Craterus, now led the main body of the Greek army from its camp, across the river, and toward Porus's rear. Porus was forced to split up his army to guard both sides; this proved disastrous for the Indians. When Alexander's forces charged forward, Porus's men were overwhelmed and forced to immediately retreat to the lines of their war elephants.

Using showers of spears and arrows, the Greeks forced many of the huge animals back into the Indian ranks, where they did a great deal of damage, and the rest of Porus's army fled. The significance of Porus's loss is clear from the casualty reports described by Arrian:

> Nearly 20,000 of the Indian infantry were killed ... and about 3,000 of their cavalry. All their war chariots were destroyed. Among the dead were two sons of Porus ... The surviving elephants were captured. Out of Alexander's original 6,000 infantry, some eighty were killed; in addition to these he lost ten of the mounted archers, who were the first unit to engage ... and 200 of the other cavalry.[15]

Porus, raja of Paurava, refused to simply turn over his lands to Alexander the Great. Shown here is the famous battle between the two powerful leaders.

Following the battle, a wounded Porus met with Alexander. Alexander was so impressed with Porus's courage and dignity that he restored him to his throne; of course, part of the deal was that Paurava was now a Greek ally that would follow Alexander's orders and supply him with troops and supplies. Arrian wrote the two men had great respect for one another and became lifelong friends.

A STOPPING POINT

Even after proving his military strength, Alexander had to rely on Pauravan resources for his ongoing campaign in India. The famous warrior king needed large amounts of supplies to support his troops in their continued eastward march. Alexander was not satisfied with past victories; he planned to conquer the rest of India. In particular, he had set his sights on seizing the great east-Indian kingdom of Magadha, whose riches and power attracted him. Rumors that Magadha had an army considerably bigger and more lethal than those in Paurava—which turned out to be true—spread through the Greek ranks. Alexander's men were already exhausted from years of marching and fighting far from home. The projected invasion of Magadha was, for them, the proverbial last straw. Upon reaching the Hyphasis River (now the Beas), they simply refused to march any further east.

The End of a Campaign

Though Alexander had marched successfully through much of India, he eventually had to turn toward home because of low support among his troops. After the most successful and prolific military career in human record, Alexander died in the Mesopotamian city of Babylon at the age of 33, less than 3 years after returning. Most of the lands he had taken in the Punjab were reclaimed by the Magadhan army his men had been reluctant to face. However, Bactria and other nearby lands that Alexander had conquered remained in Greek hands. In the years that followed, many thousands of Greek farmers, merchants, artisans, and others settled in the areas that are now northern Afghanistan and Pakistan.

At first, these Greek-ruled areas owed allegiance to one of Alexander's successors, Seleucus I, who also ruled Mesopotamia and Iran. As Seleucus and his successors became involved in wars in the western part of their realm, their hold on Bactria weakened. In about 250 BC, the Bactrian Greeks broke away from the Seleucid Empire and established a Greco-Bactrian kingdom. That same pattern was repeated three generations later: in about 180 BC, Demetrius, son of the Greco-Bactrian king Euthydemus I, invaded India. In a mere five years, Demetrius and his general, Menander, succeeded in conquering the entire Indus Valley and some regions beyond it. Soon afterward, they broke away from the Greco-Bactrian kingdom and instead established their own realm, an Indo-Greek kingdom. Menander, who rose from general to king after the death of Demetrius, proved to be the greatest of a series of Indo-Greek kings who ruled until about 10 BC.

Cross-Cultural Pollination

Greek cultural influences introduced into India in these centuries were considerable and long-lasting. They were part of a hybrid Greco-Indian culture in which ideas and customs flowed both ways between Greeks and Indians. Menander converted to Buddhism, for instance, as did many other Indo-Greeks. Similarly, Greek coinage styles spread across India and remained in use for many centuries. A number of Greek words, including those for "book," "pen," "ink," and several military terms, permanently entered Sanskrit.

Particularly important were Greek artistic influences, which produced the hybrid Greco-Buddhist style of sculpture. Greeks and Indians, either trained by Greeks or imitating them, created finely crafted busts and statues of Buddha. These works showed him with wavy hair, draped cloaks, sandals, and carved decorations featuring acanthus leaves, all Greek artistic motifs. Although Buddha was a prophet rather than a god, Greek sculptors had a strong tradition of carved statues of gods. The new style portrayed Buddha as something in between: a kind of demigod. This image of Buddhism's founder was subsequently adopted by other Asian peoples, including the Chinese and the inhabitants of Japan.

From 326 BC to 10 BC, Greeks ruled large portions of western India and nearby lands and created a lasting cultural heritage in the region. They were unable to penetrate other parts of the subcontinent, however, where native Indians held firm political power. A mere two years after Alexander's death, a new dynasty arose in Magadha. The members of this ruling family were destined to forge a realm that would dwarf all that had come before it in India.

CHAPTER FOUR

THE RISE OF MAGADHA

Because the Persian and Greek intrusions into India were concentrated in the West, many eastern kingdoms experienced little direct or immediate negative effects; in fact, the powerful kingdom of Magadha was able to leverage the weakened state of the western nations to amass both power and wealth. Even before the foreign invasions, a dynasty of Magadhan rulers—the Nandas—assembled a very large army, which they used to expand their holdings and influence in the region. This martial might also established Magadha as a significant power in the subcontinent.

The dynasty that followed in Magadha, the Mauryan, inherited that huge military establishment. Employing both a massive army and considerable political skills, the Mauryans built on the foundations their predecessors had laid, achieving a level of success that far surpassed the impressive achievements of the Nanda dynasty. The Mauryan Empire eventually encompassed almost the entire Indian subcontinent—an unprecedented accomplishment. It was the most expansive Indian empire in history, and historians have claimed that it was not only large, but also ruled by powerful figures.

India's First Emperor

Magadha was already the most influential kingdom in eastern India at the time the Nandas came to power under their first and greatest ruler, Mahapadma Nanda. The exact date of the dynasty's beginnings is uncertain. This is partly because only a few ancient Indian sources from that era have survived, and most of these sources differ on the date in question, as well as on the years of Mahapadma's reign. Some modern scholars estimate that he took the Magadhan throne around 424 BC and ruled until about 362 BC, while other experts favor a shorter alternative timeline for the Nanda period. This theory identifies the start of his reign around 380 BC.

Whenever he actually lived and ruled, Mahapadma Nanda is often considered India's first historical emperor. He and the heirs that followed him—sons and perhaps even grandsons—were certainly the subcontinent's first would-be empire-builders. Like many ancient figures, very little of a personal nature is known about the Nanda family, although some brief facts about Mahapadma appear in both ancient Indian and ancient western sources. A startling detail from these sources is that Mahapadma was the first Indian king born of a low caste. According to the first century AD Roman historian Quintus Curtius Rufus,

[Mahapadma's father] had been a barber whose regular employment barely kept starvation at bay, but by his good looks he won the heart of the queen. By her he had been brought into a comparatively close friendship with the king of the time, whom he then treacherously murdered, seizing the throne ... He then killed the [king's] children.[16]

Some local sources add that Mahapadma's low birth outraged rulers in neighboring kingdoms, who were all members of the Kshatriya caste. The caste system—still widely prevalent throughout India—breaks society into four broad classes: the Brahmins (priests), the Kshatriyas (rulers, politicians, and warriors), the Vaishyas (farmers and merchants), and the Sudras (laborers). For a member of the Sudra caste to rise to the position of king had never been done before. Furious that Mahapadma was breaking society's rules, members of the Kshatriya accused him of destroying ancient traditions.

These words turned out to be prophetic. Once he had risen to power, Mahapadma turned a destructive eye to most of the princes who had insulted him. After carefully and skillfully organizing a large military force, he invaded and seized control of several neighboring states. The exact size of the territories he overran is unknown, but some of his immediate successors built on his conquests. At its peak, the Nanda Empire covered a large portion of northern India, stretching from the Bay of Bengal in the East to the outer edges of the Indus Valley in the West.

Mahapadma's formidable army would benefit not only Mahapadma himself, but his descendants as well. Mahapadma's successors were able to build on and maintain this empire thanks to the military might assembled under India's first Sudra king. The army was so great, in fact, that when it was under the command of the last Nanda king, Dhana Nanda, it was such a feared military force that Alexander the Great's men refused to fight against it. According to some historical sources, the army consisted of 80,000 cavalrymen, 200,000 infantrymen, 8,000 chariots, and 6,000 war elephants.

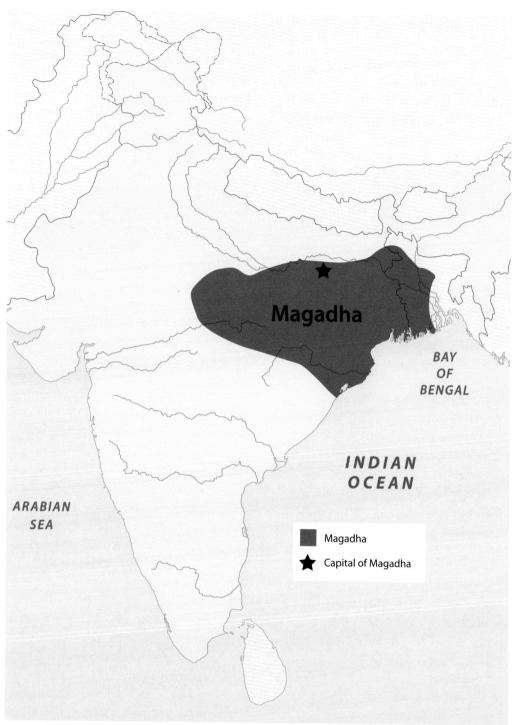

Magadha was India's first true empire.

These figures were undoubtedly exaggerated. The slightly more modest figures quoted by Quintus Curtius Rufus—20,000 cavalrymen, 200,000 infantrymen, 2,000 chariots, and 3,000 elephants—may also be too high. However, even if the Magadhan army was only half as large as Quintus Curtius Rufus reported, it was still enormous by ancient standards; it is no surprise that the Greeks were not eager to engage in battle against it.

The Rise of a Rebel King

Though largely successful in conquest, domestic life in the Nanda Empire was far more troubled. Historical record from the time reports widespread governmental corruption, court scandal, murder within the royal family, and increasing discontent among the populace. Rising tension created an atmosphere ripe for a charismatic and ambitious individual to step in and seize the moment.

Sometime in the early 320s BC, a man from the Vaishya caste, Chandragupta Maurya, joined forces with a Brahmin named Kautilya. The latter, once a member of the Nanda court, had recently fallen out of favor with Dhana Nanda. Chandragupta and Kautilya tried to overthrow the emperor, but were unsuccessful and had to flee.

The two schemers remained undaunted, however. They and a core group of followers amassed an army of disgruntled citizens from various outlying regions of the Nanda realm. Soon,

they staged a second, larger coup. After overrunning "the outlying provinces of the Nanda kingdom," John Keay wrote, the rebels eventually converged on Magadha:

> [The capital of] Pataliputra was probably besieged and, aided no doubt by defectors, the [rebels] triumphed. The last Nanda was sent packing, quite literally: he is supposed to have been spared only his life, plus [any] of his legendary wealth as he could crate and carry away ... and Chandragupta Maurya ascended the Magadhan throne.[17]

Chandragupta Maurya was around 25 years old when he took power in Magadha, and he had no experience as a national leader. However, from the start of his rule, he proved himself a skilled and effective leader. This was almost certainly due to the advice he continued to get from his friend and confidant, Kautilya, a political theorist. Kautilya wrote a book on statecraft titled the *Arthashastra* (meaning "Science of Material Gain"), which has survived. It describes an effective ruler as one who takes an active role in all government affairs and puts the good of the country and citizenry above his own. "If a king is energetic, his subjects will be equally energetic," Kautilya wrote. By contrast,

> If he is reckless, they will not only be reckless likewise, but also eat into his works. Besides, a reckless king will

Chandragupta is one of the most influential leaders in Indian history. Shown here is a gold dinar coin featuring Chandragupta on the right.

easily fall into the hands of his enemies … In the happiness of his subjects lies his happiness; in their welfare his welfare; whatever pleases himself he shall not consider as good, but whatever pleases his subjects he shall consider as good. Hence the king shall ever be active and discharge his duties; the root of wealth is activity, and of evil its reverse.[18]

Chandragupta seems to have done his best to live by these words. The fourth-century Greek writer Megasthenes, who lived for some time in the Mauryan court, said that the Indian raja was a tireless and attentive ruler:

He then remains in court for the whole day without allowing the business to be interrupted, even though the hour arrives when he [is required to] attend to his person … The palace is open to all comers, even when the king is having his hair combed and dressed. It is then that he gives audience to ambassadors, and administers justice to his subjects.[19]

Struggle and Peace

It was not by chance that the Greek Megasthenes found himself at the Mauryan court in India. His arrival was the culmination of a series of tactical moves by Chandragupta and his enormous inherited army.

Similarly to the Nanda rajas before him, Chandragupta was not content to rule over the territory he already had.

His vision for Magadha was much bigger. Shortly after taking Magadha's throne, Chandragupta took advantage of the formidable army he had inherited from the Nandas and launched several large-scale military expeditions. By about 311 BC, he had gained control of all the land stretching from Magadha westward to the Indus River, including some of the territories Alexander had brought under Greek control only two decades before. In fact, Chandragupta's chief Greek opponent in the struggle for these territories was Alexander's former general Seleucus, who now controlled Mesopotamia, Iran, Bactria, and parts of the western Indus Valley.

After some bloody fighting—in which the Mauryians seem to have gotten the upper hand—the two sides agreed to make peace. Chandragupta (whom the Greeks called Sandrocottus) and Seleucus signed a treaty in 305 BC. In it, the Greek king ceded a large section of former Greek lands west of the Indus to Chandragupta, in exchange for a number of military assets and a dynastic alliance. This meant that the two families would marry one of their members to the other, which would tie the two sides together formally. Either a Greek princess married a Mauryan prince or a Mauryan princess married a Greek prince; the ancient sources are unclear on this point. Seleucus sent Megasthenes as his ambassador to the Mauryan court. There, Megasthenes learned about the traditions, culture, and expectations of the Indian court, lessons which would later appear in a book titled *Indika*. Small sections of this work have survived as quotes in the books of later ancient writers.

During the course of his reign, Chandragupta was able to realize more of his vision of a vast Magadhan kingdom than any other ruler before him. His conquests were spectacular and effective. Eventually, his court held sway over almost all of northern India, causing later western writers to call him the "Indian Julius Caesar," in reference to the famous Roman general who conquered Gaul (what is now France).

An Abrupt Abandonment

Chandragupta would most likely have pressed on with his army and expanded Magadha's holdings further, if not for the strange and sudden way in which his rule came to an end. The rich kingdom of Kalinga, lying south of Magadha, was still independent, as were the Deccan kingdoms; it is reasonable to assume that a conquering king such as Chandragupta would have set his sights on bringing them under the Magadhan banner. In 297 BC, however, Chandragupta did something exceedingly rare: He abdicated his throne, became a poor Jain monk, and starved himself to death.

Despite historical sources confirming his actions, scholars have questioned whether Chandragupta truly gave up his rule and died. They have wondered why a powerful, successful raja would abdicate at the height of his power, while still relatively young and with all the opportunity in the world. These scholars suspect that Chandragupta's son, Bindusara, who became raja upon his father's abdication, somehow assassinated his father and came up with a cover story about his father abdicating and moving south to pursue his holy calling. Still, there are other experts, such as Vincent Arthur Smith, who accept the official story as the true one:

The only direct evidence throwing light on the manner in which the eventful reign of the Chandragupta Maurya came to an end is that of Jain tradition. The Jains always treat the great emperor as having been a Jain … and no adequate reason seems to exist for discrediting their belief … Once the fact that Chandragupta was or became a Jain is admitted, the tradition that he abdicated and committed suicide by slow starvation in the approved Jain manner becomes readily credible.[20]

In whatever manner Bindusara gained the throne, he reigned until around 272 BC, a total of about 25 years. Little of a concrete nature is known about his personal life, but there is no question that, like his father, he was an ambitious and skilled soldier. Bindusara expanded the empire by conquering large portions of the Deccan.

Megasthenes arriving in India has been depicted in works of art ranging from paintings to comic books, such as the artist's impression shown here.

The Sorrowless One

By the end of Bindusara's reign, the Mauryan Empire was bigger than any native Indian nation or empire had ever been. It was destined to grow still larger under his son and successor, Aśoka (sometimes written as Ashoka). Many modern scholars consider Aśoka to be the greatest of the Mauryan rajas.

Aśoka's rule had a shaky start. When Bindusara died, he left behind several sons, all of whom believed they had the right to the throne. According to the *Divyadana*, an ancient Buddhist anthology, Bindusaura had planned for his oldest son, Susima, to inherit the throne. Important government officials, on the other hand, preferred Aśoka (whose name means "The Sorrowless One"). It is difficult to say exactly what occurred during the interim between Bindusaura's death and Aśoka's victory, as most documentation takes the form of religious or mythological texts, rather than historical record. Two texts, the *Dipavamsa* and the *Mahavamsa*, suggest that Aśoka killed 99 of 100 brothers, sparing only his favorite, Vitashoka. Though it seems unlikely that the story unfolded exactly like this, it is true that Aśoka emerged victorious in the fight for the throne and became raja sometime in the early-to-mid 260s BC.

From the start, the young emperor was determined to conquer the only important kingdom in India not yet under Mauryan control: Kalinga. Not long after ascending to the throne, he launched a full-scale invasion of Kalinga, whose inhabitants were completely overwhelmed. Ancient sources describe an enormous bloodbath in which 100,000 were killed, tens of thousands more were captured or driven from their homes, and thousands died of illness or starvation in the months that followed.

Then, as with his grandfather Chandragupta, something extraordinary happened to Aśoka: Having attained his most cherished goal and become the most powerful man in India's history, he had a change of heart. When he beheld the bodies of the dead and witnessed the terrible suffering of the shattered families and communities, he was horrified and deeply remorseful. Moreover, he had the courage and depth of character to admit it to all his subjects. Aśoka ordered messages inscribed on rocks and pillars across his empire, saying in part:

[I am] deeply pained by the killing, dying and deportation that take place when an unconquered country is conquered. But [I am] pained even more [when that country's people] are injured, killed or separated from their loved ones. Even those who are not affected (by all this) suffer when they see friends, acquaintances, companions and relatives affected. These misfortunes befall all (as a result of war), and this pains [me] … Therefore the killing, death or deportation of a hundredth, or even a thousandth part of those who died during the conquest of Kalinga now pains [me].[21]

Aśoka's Change of Heart

In keeping with this new, more humane philosophy, Aśoka converted to Buddhism, which teaches followers to act nonviolently, among many other things. Across his vast empire, he instituted the Buddhist concept of dharma (also spelled dhamma), which is essentially a set of moral guidelines or laws. Aśoka's interpretation of dharma was that all people should be kind and generous, avoiding cruelty and aggression, to achieve a peaceful and happy life.

Ruling within the constraints of dharma, Aśoka forbade the slaughter of animals, which significantly reduced meat eating in India. He also promoted Buddhism by sending missionaries far and wide to spread the faith's nonviolent beliefs and other ideologies. Alongside this policy, however, he urged religious tolerance, saying that all faiths are worthy of respect. He issued advice that it was always best to respect other religions while still maintaining personal faith.

In addition, Aśoka tried to improve his people's welfare by creating hospitals, roads, fountains, and gardens. Finally, he adhered to the *Arthashastra*'s principles of fair and efficient government introduced during his grandfather's reign.

CUSTOMS OF THE DHARMA

In this passage from one of Aśoka's rock inscriptions, he lists some of the ceremonies, or customs, of the dharma and explains why they are superior to other customs.

> The ceremony of the Dhamma … involves proper behavior towards servants and employees, respect for teachers, restraint towards living beings, and generosity towards [religious officials]. These and other things constitute the ceremony of the Dhamma. Therefore a father, a son, a brother, a master, a friend, a companion, and even a neighbor should say: "This is good, this is the ceremony that should be performed until its purpose is fulfilled, this I shall do." Other ceremonies are of doubtful fruit, for they may achieve their purpose, or they may not, and even if they do, it is only in this world. But the ceremony of the Dhamma is timeless.[1]

1. Aśoka, "The Edicts of King Asoka," Ven S. Dhammika, trans., The Edicts of King Ashoka, accessed July 13, 2017. www.cs.colostate.edu/~malaiya/ashoka.html.

The End of an Empire

Unfortunately for Aśoka's subjects, his successors were far less capable than he was. For the most part, all seven rajas who occupied the Mauryan throne following his death in the 230s BC lacked his vision, skills, sense of humanity, and sheer boldness of leadership. As a result, they were able to maintain neither the respect of their people nor the integrity of the realm. The empire steadily shrank as rebellions erupted and its outlying provinces broke away and declared their independence. The dynasty came to an inglorious end in 185 BC, when the commander of the army assassinated the last Mauryan ruler, Brihadratha.

Though the Mauryans were gone, they left behind a formidable legacy, parts of which helped shape the character of India in later ages. Indeed, the cohesion of most of the Indian subcontinent into one nation would become an inspiration for Indians in the coming centuries—but would not be realized again until modern times. As Keay wrote, "the ideal of a pan-Indian empire was never forgotten."[22]

The four-headed lion, Aśoka's chosen symbol, represented power, courage, pride, and confidence.

Perhaps the biggest and most profound aspect of the Mauryan legacy, though, was Aśoka's support of Buddhism. His missionaries traveled not only to every section of the subcontinent, but also into neighboring lands. As a result, the faith eventually spread across all of eastern Asia and became one of the world's great religions.

Aśoka's policy of religious tolerance also allowed Hinduism and Jainism to remain strong in India, and both faiths continued to gain followers. Indeed, it is remarkable that not long before the Mauryans' rise to power, India had produced three major religions that would survive for thousands of years. Moreover, this achievement, one of the most important contributions made to world culture by any nation, had occurred in the amazingly short span of a few centuries.

GODS AND MEN

The three major religions that originated on the Indian subcontinent and spread worldwide—Jainism, Buddhism, and Hinduism—are among the most significant products of ancient India. These faiths have proven to be powerful, even over the course of more than 2,000 years, and have billions of modern followers between them. The most prominent religion for Indians in the 21st century is Hinduism, which has come directly from Vedic traditions and beliefs. The ancient Vedic faith, which has its roots in the third millennium BC, was adapted and developed over hundreds of years until an early form of Hinduism emerged around the time of the Mahājanapadas in the first century BC.

Because the Vedic faith had strong foundations and a rich history of change and refinement, it continued to spread after being identified as Hinduism. Moreover, because the religion was so open to new ideas and practices, countless new belief systems were allowed to rise right alongside it. Some of these new concepts and beliefs inspired the emergence of Buddhism and Jainism, beginning around 500 BC. These faiths did not reject Vedic-Hindu religious traditions directly. Instead, they incorporated and adjusted many of them into their own systems. Though Buddhism largely disappeared from India later, partly as a result of large-scale Muslim invasions, the three faiths coexisted in the subcontinent for centuries.

Faith and Custom in the Vedic Era

Hinduism, Buddhism, and Jainism all have their roots in the even older

Vedic faith, but details about how and when this ancient religion began are unclear. The precise beliefs and rituals of the early Vedic faith are also uncertain, although some aspects of it still exist in Hindu worship. What seems clear is that over the course of many centuries, the Vedic religion underwent slow but steady change.

A long evolution in religious concepts and rituals can be seen in the adoption of new gods over time. In each instance, the older gods were not discarded; instead, priests and worshippers assigned them less prominent roles in the cosmic and spiritual order, or rita. Dyaus was the first primary deity in the Vedic faith. Roughly equivalent to the Greek Zeus, he was a sky god who could control the weather and command the forces of thunder and lightning. A few of the hymns in the Rigveda mention him, but by the time these hymns were composed, he was no longer the main god.

As time went on, Dyaus was demoted to the role of a more distant divine father-figure, and his son, Varuna, became the most significant deity. Although he was a sky god like his father, Varuna also oversaw the underworld. The Rigveda pictures Varuna as both supremely holy and wise, as well as powerful. One hymn says in part:

[Varuna] knows the path of birds
* that fly through heaven …*
He knows the pathway of the wind,
* the spreading, high, and*
* mighty wind:*
*   He knows the Gods who*
*   dwell above.*
Varuna, true to holy law, sits
* down among his people; he,*
*   Most wise, sits there to*
*   govern all.*
From [there] perceiving he beholds
* all wondrous things, both what*
* hath been,*
*   And what hereafter will*
*   be done.*[23]

Eventually, the Vedic faith adopted another of Dyaus's sons, Indra, as its primary god. In Vedic myths, Indra defeated a powerful demon of drought named Vritra, thereby allowing sunlight and water to invigorate the earth and make human life possible. Worship of Indra and the other Vedic gods did not take place in temples, which appeared later in India. Instead, hearth-like altars were erected to accommodate the main ritual of worship: fire sacrifices. Guided by the fire god Agni, Brahmin priests led people in lighting sacred fires and chanting hymns, acts that were meant to appease the gods and purify the worshippers.

Agni, the fire god, had two heads and was often depicted as sitting on a ram, a typical symbol of sacrifice.

Brahma and the *Ishvara*

As early Hinduism emerged, it retained hymn-chanting, fire rituals, and other aspects of Vedic worship. However, the Hindus added some important new concepts. First, they introduced a creator-god—Brahma, who was also the basis for a different way of thinking about the gods in general. The older Vedic gods had been part of a traditional polytheistic belief system, in which people worshipped several separate divine entities.

In contrast, a majority of ancient Hindus came to view Brahma as a sort of supreme, universal spirit, called the *ishvara* (or *ishwara*). This spirit had the ability to manifest itself in different ways, taking on various alternate faces and forms. Among these forms were other Hindu gods, including Shiva, god of destruction; Vishnu, the preserver and governor of the universe; and Ganesh, the elephant-headed god of wisdom and learning. Similarly, each of these deities could manifest in different forms. Vishnu, for example, took several earthly guises or incarnations, among them Rama (who appears in the *Ramayana*) and Krishna (a major character in the *Bhagavad-Gita*, a part of the *Mahabharata*). In addition to these various divine manifestations, the Hindus recognized a number of separate heavenly beings. These included the *devas*, somewhat equivalent to angels, and the Asuras, or demons. Ancient Hinduism intricately combined various aspects of monotheism and polytheism.

Ancient Hinduism also placed a strong emphasis on the concept of reincarnation (samsara), or repeated rebirth of the human soul (the atman). The belief was that the soul is immortal. When someone's body died, the soul passed into another body, and this process repeated itself as the soul strived to better itself and become one with the universal spirit. The circumstances and experiences of each successive lifetime were dependent on Karma, a strict law of moral consequences. A term familiar even to non-Hindus, Karma is a measure of someone's good and bad actions. Helping a stranger could generate positive Karma, while stealing could generate negative Karma. As the two sides accumulated throughout a person's life, Hindus believed that their next life would reflect their total balance.

These concepts reinforced the caste system, which divided people into groups of varying status, moral worth, and level of material comforts. Someone who generated a lot of negative Karma in one lifetime could be expected to be born into a lower caste in the next life—while those who did good deeds looked forward to rising up the caste system. To establish oneself as a good person, worshippers had to demonstrate their devotion to through regular performance of standard rituals of worship (puja). This could be done in a temple with the aid of priests. In fact, erecting large, elaborately decorated temples was seen as a way of showing people's dedication to divine forces and righteous living.

Worshippers could also perform the rituals at home using small makeshift shrines. These most often featured icons (*murti*)—statues or paintings symbolizing chosen gods. The rituals included chanting, placing food offerings on the shrine, reading from the Vedas, *Ramayana*, or other Hindu scriptures, lighting candles, burning incense, and meditation.

Buddha and Enlightenment

Like the Hindus, the ancient Buddhists had temples, priests, scriptures, and beliefs in the existence of various heavenly beings. However, Buddhists viewed these beings not as controllers of the cosmic order but simply as parts of it, making them equally subject to its laws. Furthermore, early Buddhists did not recognize an all-powerful creator-god. A philosophy and way of understanding life, as well as a religion, Buddhism became a path to the discovery of knowledge and peace with oneself, one's community, and the larger universe. A Buddhist could find that path with the aid of priests, but they could also do it alone, as an individual seeking salvation through the attainment of wisdom. In that way, each person had the potential to become an instrument of their own fate.

Buddhism was based on the life and teachings of a man who became known

EVOLVING BUDDHIST ART

Those ancient peoples who adopted the Buddha's philosophy were often inspired to celebrate the faith and its ideas in art, including sculpture. At first, it was considered disrespectful to carve statues, or icons, showing the Buddha's specific physical form. In this phase of Buddhist sculpture, which was called aniconic, artisans instead carved objects indirectly associated with the great prophet. These included the wheel of law, an important Buddhist image, which depicted the great truths Buddha had discovered; sculptures of a sacred tree, beneath which the Buddha found enlightenment; and casts of feet and footprints symbolizing the spread of Buddhist ideas far and wide. By the first century AD, however, it was no longer considered forbidden to show images of Buddha. In the centuries that followed, peoples across the Far East carved or cast statues of Buddha—some of them gigantic. In China, Japan, and other areas of the Far East, Buddhist themes combined with and complemented traditional ones in sculpture and other forms of artistic expression.

The wheel of law, shown here, has grown to be one of the iconic symbols of Buddhism.

as the Buddha, a title meaning "the enlightened one." Though he is a major historical figure, the actual details of his life are shrouded in mystery and legend. Parts of the story that developed about him in Indian tradition may be largely historically accurate, while other parts are likely exaggerated or made up. The story begins with his birth as Siddhartha Gautama, a prince in one of India's northern kingdoms. The traditional date for this event is 563 BC, but many modern scholars suspect he was born somewhat later, perhaps about 500 BC.

As a child and young man, Siddhartha led the happy, comfortable life of a royal person. His comfortable existence did not expose him to the harsher realities of life, and he knew nothing of disease, suffering, or death. However, he left the palace as an adult and began exploring the countryside. There, to his shock and dismay, he witnessed old age and its infirmities, sickness, and death and learned that these are normal, inevitable aspects of life.

This experience changed Siddhartha's life forever. He devoted himself to solitude and meditation, as Hindu monks did. Adopting an existence of extreme self-discipline and self-denial, he neglected and punished his body, hoping this would help his mind to focus better on finding life's truths. Eventually, Siddhartha came to realize that abusing his body was pointless and unproductive, as suffering only clouded his thinking.

The End of Suffering

Although he rejected the idea that suffering led to enlightenment, Siddhartha sensed that identifying the causes of suffering and learning how to reduce it were the keys to attaining true wisdom. He searched for a long time, and then one day, he had an epiphany, or sudden realization. He saw that there are four fundamental truths surrounding human existence that he called the Four Noble Truths: first, that life is filled with suffering; second, that suffering is the result of arrogance, self-indulgence, and greed; third, that these ills are not inevitable and can be overcome; and fourth, that suffering can be relieved.

This fourth and most profound truth revealed by the Buddha included the methods by which people could overcome the causes of suffering. It was a code of conduct that he called the Eightfold Path. The eight steps in the path are: correct views, correct aspiration, correct speech, correct behavior, correct vocation, correct effort, correct thoughts, and correct contemplation. According to this path, people should not kill any living thing. Nor should they steal, lie, get drunk, or have sex outside of marriage. By strictly following these steps and good behaviors, the Buddha advocated, one could attain Nirvana, which is a state of selflessness, peace, and happiness. One would also escape from the relentless cycle of reincarnation.

The Buddha went out and preached these ideas, which became increasingly popular. Many Hindus had no problem bringing together the concepts of right living and meditation with existing Hindu doctrines. Many of the Buddha's followers accepted basic Buddhist doctrines without giving up all of their former beliefs. This helped contribute to the ongoing continuity in Indian thought and society.

Well after the Buddha's death, during the reign of the Mauryan ruler Aśoka, Buddhist missionaries carried these ideas beyond India's borders, eventually helping to spread Buddhism to present-day China, Cambodia, Thailand, Korea, and Japan. As had been the case with many Indian Hindus, these foreign peoples often found ways to accept Buddhist philosophy while retaining some of their former religious beliefs.

Mahavira and the Liberation of the Soul

Like Buddhism, escaping the remorseless cycle of reincarnation and achieving liberation and ultimate knowledge were also basic beliefs of Jainism. The key figure in the early days of Jainism, Vardhamana (also known as Mahavira, meaning "Great Hero") was a contemporary of the Buddha, although it is unclear which man began preaching first. Similarly to Siddhartha, Mahavira started out as a prince leading a privileged life. He too gave up his worldly life at about the age of 30, began living a monk-like existence of self-discipline and self-denial, and eventually underwent an intellectual and spiritual transformation.

Mahavira's enlightenment consisted of his understanding that all life is potentially divine. This idea suggests that all living things, not just humans, have souls. Therefore, it is wrong to kill not only people, but also animals and even insects. Those souls could escape the cycle of reincarnation by achieving the liberation (moksha) of their souls. To do this, one's soul had to be taken away from the Karma system. Unlike the Hindus and Buddhists, the Jains viewed Karma as the material from which the universe is made, and the goal was to escape from Karma's grip and reach a heavenly level above and beyond it. There, souls would become siddhas, or beings without suffering and ignorance.

This process of liberation, which had many similarities to Buddhism, could be accomplished only by following certain disciplines and righteous acts. Jains believed that throughout history, Jinas (also called tirthankaras) appeared. These were special humans who had achieved enlightenment and gained ultimate knowledge, and they taught ordinary people the proper behaviors to achieve enlightenment. Jains believed that Mahavira was one of the Jinas. He taught two sets of vows, or rules of right behavior. The first, a code known as the mahavratas (or "great vows"), were for Jain monks, who led more disciplined lives than average believers. These vows included rules against violence, lying, or taking anything that has not been offered freely. The other set of vows, mostly targeted toward regular followers, were called anuvratas (or "lesser vows"). These were less strict, and the most important was a vow against eating meat or destroying life.

Six occupations emerged that were considered acceptable for Jains to adopt: farming, government work, writing, artistic endeavors, crafting, and commerce. Like Buddhism, Jainism held wide appeal for Indians at the time, and the new belief system spread steadily through the subcontinent. At first, Jain ideals were taught by Mahavira's disciples, who collected his teachings into the earliest Jain scriptures. Among them are the Kalpa-sūtra (Book of Ritual) and the Tattvārthā-sutra (Book of Reality). In the Jain philosophy contained in these

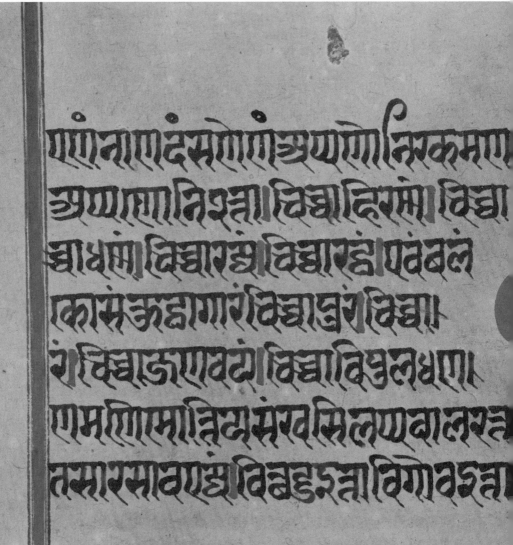

writings, liberated souls attained a pure state of infinite knowledge, perception, and happiness. Like Buddhism, Jainism had no universal creator-god. Most Jains did acknowledge the existence of the Hindu deities, but they saw these gods as subject to the same natural laws and processes as humans, including reincarnation and the quest for liberation.

By the time of the rise of the Mauryan Empire in the late fourth century BC, India had a complex and largely accepting religious culture. Basic Hindu beliefs had been greatly enriched by Buddhist and Jain philosophical ideas, and feelings of religious tolerance pervaded society. This openness to new ideas encouraged the formation of differing schools of thought within all three faiths during the centuries that followed, including the golden age that began in the fourth century AD.

Like the Buddha, Mahavira (shown here) achieved enlightenment after giving away all his earthly possessions and dedicating himself to a spiritual life.

CHAPTER SIX

THE GOLDEN AGE OF GUPTAS

After the fall of the Mauryan Empire in 185 BC, India entered a new political era. Where unity had ruled under strong, charismatic leaders such as Chandragupta and Aśoka, now local dynasties and territories rose and fell. This period, ruled by what scholars call the Middle Kingdoms, was divided sharply along territorial lines: Magadha, ruled by the Shunga (or Sunga) dynasty; Kalinga, which had broken free from Magadha and re-established its independence; the Indo-Grecian region established by the Bactrian Greeks Demetrius and Menander; several kingdoms in the Deccan; and a series of dynasties of central Asian origin that ruled in the subcontinent's northwestern sector. It was not until AD 300, when the Gupta dynasty united northern India, that political stability returned to the region.

Although the Gupta Empire was never as expansive as the Mauryan, its legacy is just as significant. Where Mauryan rulers had craved expansion and military might, the Gupta Empire is remembered for its success in another way. The Guptas reigned over an age of widespread peace and prosperity, and their rulers championed the arts and sciences. The era's artistic and literary flowering, along with advances in mathematics, astronomy, philosophy, medicine, and other intellectual endeavors, inspired modern historians to call it India's cultural golden age.

Life After the Mauryans

Though the Gupta period boasted major political unity, prosperity, and cultural achievements, the time of the earlier Middle Kingdoms was far from a dark age. To the contrary, though politically disunited and often war-torn, most of these pre-Gupta states were quite prosperous and culturally rich. The Shunga dynasty in Magadha is a clear illustration. Its founder, Pushyamitra Shunga, was the Magadhan military general who assassinated the last Mauryan ruler. He and his successors, who ruled for a little more than a century, frequently warred with the Kalingans, the Indo-Greeks, and others. Still, trade went on all across India, producing much of the wealth that financed these conflicts. The Shungas sponsored many cultural achievements as well, including education, literature, fine arts, and the building of many splendid Buddhist temples. Moreover, many of these programs continued under the next Magadhan dynasty—the Kanva. The Kanvas overthrew the Shungas in 72 BC and ruled the country for roughly 50 years.

Meanwhile, northwestern India, including the Indus Valley, endured an influx of foreign rulers beginning in the early first century BC. First came the Shakas (or Sakas), which modern scholars sometimes call the Indo-Scythians. The Shakas came from central Asia and destroyed the Greek Bactrian kingdom on their way into India. Not long afterward, the Yuezhi, who came to be called the Kushans, displaced the Shaka kings. Some of the Shakas moved into the southern Indus Valley and ruled there for several centuries.

However, the idea of a large-scale Kushan invasion of India—implying major population movements and disruptions—must be viewed with caution. As John Keay pointed out, "India's ancient history was first reconstructed largely by British scholars in the nineteenth century, who, schooled on the invasions of Aryans, Macedonians and Muslims [in India's medieval period], readily detected a pattern of incursions."[24] Thus, although some kind of Kushan invasion may well have occurred, it is also possible that the Kushans were brought into the subcontinent as mercenary soldiers for an Indian kingdom or arrived as refugees fleeing their own homelands.

Regardless of how they initially got there, after the Kushans arrived in western India, they acquired political control, converted to Buddhism, and became eager patrons of the arts and literature. However, the Kushans were not interested in imposing their own styles and perspectives on their newly conquered people. They promoted and provided the money for the creation of numerous paintings and large statues of the Buddha, while still allowing the ongoing merger of native Indian and Greek artistic styles to prevail. The result was a unique and fruitful joint artistic effort among members of three quite different cultures. The Kushans, Keay wrote, controlled

east–west trade in Bactria as well as vast territories in India, had wealth to lavish on both the new faith [Buddhism] and the new art ... The style developed rapidly, influencing architecture and painting, and inspiring a narrative art based on Buddhist legend but using Graeco-Roman compositions and mannerisms. Exceptionally, the figure of the Buddha himself ...

conformed strictly to Indo-Buddhist [style]. Such was the ... tradition, a curious synthesis [combination] of Kushana patronage, Graeco-Roman forms and Indian inspiration. In sculpture, stucco, engraving and painting, it was this synthesis which ... [provided] the inspiration for later Buddhist art in China and beyond.[25]

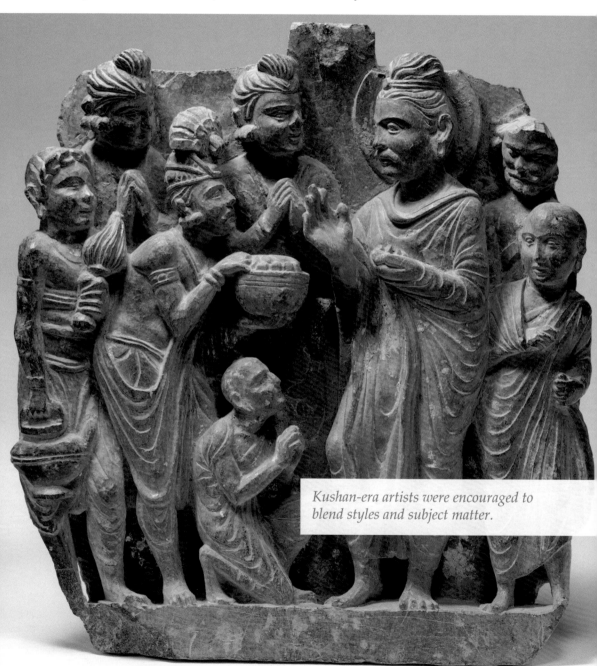

Kushan-era artists were encouraged to blend styles and subject matter.

FAXIAN MAKES A PILGRIMAGE

Faxian, a Chinese Buddhist living in the late fourth century to early fifth century AD, wrote an important historical text documenting life at the time, which he titled *A Record of Buddhistic Kingdoms*. This book chronicles his journeys through India on a pilgrimage to visit some of the original Buddhist sites, especially places where the Buddha was said to have lived. In this excerpt from the work, he describes his emotional visit to a hill on which the founder of his faith had supposedly preached:

> The hall where Buddha preached his Law has been destroyed, and only the foundations of the brick walls remain. On this hill the peak is beautifully green, and rises grandly up; it is the highest of all the five hills … [I] bought incense-(sticks), flowers, oil and lamps, and hired two [local men] to carry them (to the peak). When [I] got to it, [I] made offerings with the flowers and incense, and lighted the lamps when the darkness began to come on. [I] felt melancholy, but restrained [my] tears and said, "Here Buddha delivered [the Law]. I, [Faxian], was born when I could not meet with Buddha; and now I only see the footprints which he has left, and the place where he lived, and nothing more."[1]

1. Faxian, *A Record of Buddhistic Kingdoms*, James Legge, trans. Oxford, UK: Clarendon Press, 1886, pp. 83–84.

The Great Guptas

The Guptas rose to power in what was already a culturally rich region. Under their rule, arts and literature, as well as commerce and prosperity, flourished to an astonishing degree. The exact origins of the Guptas, as well as the manner in which they established their dynasty in Magadha, are somewhat shrouded in uncertainty. The most prevalent theory is that they were from Bengal, the region directly east of Magadha. In about AD 320, the founder of the dynasty, Chandra Gupta I (not to be confused with the Mauryan ruler of the same name) gained power in Magadha, perhaps partly by royal marriage and partly by military force.

In whatever manner he took the throne, Chandra Gupta I immediately revealed himself to be a man of enormous confidence with equally huge ambitions. He called himself king of kings and set a goal of restoring the lost glories of the Mauryan Empire. The extent of his conquests, if he made any, are unknown. In all likelihood, they were probably limited; the first major Gupta military expansion occurred under his son, Samudra Gupta, who took power around AD 330.

Samudra was even more ambitious—and successful—than his father. As king, he led large-scale military campaigns across northern India. Initially, he enjoyed considerable success, conquering territories stretching from the Punjab to the Bay of Bengal and incorporating them into his new empire. However, he faced considerable resistance elsewhere; both the Deccan kingdoms and western lands managed to resist Gupta domination.

Military might was not the whole of Samudra's ambition. A musician and poet himself, he spent large sums sponsoring other artists. Once again, Pataliputra became India's principal cultural center, marking the beginning of the cultural golden age.

Many kings during this era issued coins with their image stamped on them, adopting the practice from the Greeks and the Romans.

The Peak of Power

When Samudra Gupta died around AD 380 after a long and fruitful reign, one of his sons, Ramagupta, inherited the throne. Ramagupta would not remain in power long; his brother, Chandragupta, soon removed him and took the title Chandragupta II. The actual events of the coup are still a mystery to scholars, but dramatic retellings of the tale almost certainly contain fragments of truth.

First, as the story goes, Ramagupta attacked the western regions in a bid to bring them under the Gupta banner. However, he overstepped his power and was forced to sign an unfavorable treaty. Traditional legends claim that after this treaty, which enraged Chandragupta II, he made a plan to assassinate his brother and seize control. The plan succeeded.

Having taken control of the Gupta Empire, Chandragupta II brought it to what would turn out to be the pinnacle of power and influence. He adopted the title Vikramaditya, meaning "he who is stronger than the sun," and launched the first of several military campaigns against the western lands. The size and composition of the army he employed in these expeditions is not precisely known, but most scholars think among its mainstays was a large corps of foot archers. Archers in that era used a sturdy bamboo bow that fired bamboo arrows with metal tips to great distances. Similar to medieval English longbows, these weapons could do severe damage to columns of charging horsemen. Noblemen and other wealthy Indian archers sometimes used steel bows. Archers also carried swords, which they used only if the enemy made it through the rain of arrows and attacked them man-to-man. Some archers fired from platforms mounted atop elephants; these great beasts were also trained to charge and trample enemy infantry.

By about 409, Chandragupta II had achieved complete victory over the western subcontinent and brought all of western India under Gupta control. However, conquest was not Chandragupta II's only method of statesmanship; he allied with the remaining independent Deccan kingdoms through the marriage of one of his daughters to the strongest Deccan king, ensuring friendly relations and the extension of Gupta influence throughout the region.

This tremendously extensive unification, coupled with several years of peace, allowed the Gupta government to concentrate on expanding the economy and promoting the welfare of the citizenry. Foreign visitors during this period were amazed at the level of prosperity, which modern historians think rivaled that of the Roman Empire at its height. The Chinese Buddhist Faxian, who toured India in the early 400s, was particularly impressed by the imperial heartland of Magadha. "The cities and towns of this country," he wrote, "are the greatest of all in [India]. The inhabitants are rich and prosperous, and vie with one another in the practice of benevolence and righteousness."[26]

Not all citizens of the Gupta Empire were rich and prosperous, of course. To manage the needs of its most vulnerable, the Gupta administration established some sort of early welfare system to provide those in need with a safety net. Faxian observed,

In the cities [there are] houses for dispensing charity and medicines. All the poor and destitute in the country, orphans, widowers, and childless men, maimed people and cripples, and all who are diseased, go to those houses, and are provided with every kind of help, and doctors examine their diseases. They get the food and medicines which their cases require, and are made to feel at ease.[27]

Life in the Gupta Empire

Faxian's guide does not just describe important religious sites; rather, it reported many of the details of Guptan life and culture that he observed during his extensive travels. One of the many benefits of Faxian's diligence in recording his experience is that modern scholars are able to study the important strides made in medicine during the Gupta rule and place those strides within the context of a larger series of achievements in the arts and sciences.

Though most people often imagine ancient peoples as being less medically advanced than society today, Faxian's observations indicate otherwise. Guptan doctors became highly efficient at delivering babies by caesarean section, setting broken bones, grafting damaged skin, and other procedures that modern doctors still learn in medical school. This medical knowledge eventually passed to Arab communities situated west of India, and from there, they spread to Europe.

Medicine was not the only scientific discipline that thrived under the Guptas. Mathematics and astronomy flourished under the hands of Guptan scholars. They devised the decimal system and introduced the concept of zero during this period, which, although taken for granted today, were enormous leaps forward in mathematical thinking. These ideas later passed to the West via the Arabs. Meanwhile, Gupta astronomers calculated the length of the solar year with a degree of accuracy greater than what ancient Greek astronomers had achieved. Furthermore, much like the Greeks, the Guptas recognized that Earth is a sphere, partly by observing the planet's curved shadow on the moon's face during lunar eclipses.

In literature, a number of talented writers were active in the Gupta Age. By far the most renowned was Kalidasa, a poet and playwright whom later western experts came to call the "Indian Shakespeare." Kalidasa powerfully and effectively explored the full range of human emotion. His works explored the nature of human life, asking questions that many artistic works still grapple with today. Working in the 5th century, he became renowned around 1,000 years before Shakespeare, leading some scholars to claim that Shakespeare ought to have been known as the English Kalidasa.

The following passage from Kalidasa's long poem, *The Birth of the War God*, is just one example of his skill. It described a god's intense feelings of love for another divine being, but on a broader level, it captured the feeling of romantic passion that people in all ages and times can relate to:

> My breast is stained; I lay among
> the ashes
> Of him I loved with all a
> woman's powers;

> Now let me lie where death-fire
> flames and flashes,
> As glad as on a bed of
> budding flowers.

> Sweet Spring, thou camest oft where
> we lay sleeping
> On blossoms, I and he whose
> life is sped;
> Unto the end thy friendly
> office keeping,
> Prepare for me the last, the fiery bed.

> And fan the flame to which I
> am committed
> With southern winds; I would
> no longer stay;

> You know well how slow the
> moments flitted
> For Love, my love, when I was
> far away.[28]

EDUCATION AT NALANDA

In the enlightened intellectual climate of Gupta-ruled India, education thrived, including schools of higher learning, which were often located in large monasteries. The most famous university of the era was the one in the Buddhist monastery at Nalanda, in northeastern India. Established by King Kumara Gupta in about 450, the huge complex of temples, classrooms, and dormitories supported thousands of students and teachers. A library containing numerous ancient Asian texts was situated inside a nine-story building.

This remarkable institution attracted pupils not only from all parts of India, but also from all over Asia and the Far East. The religious ideas and traditions promoted at Nalanda strongly influenced the later development of Buddhism in Tibet, Vietnam, China, and Japan.

Kalidasa's works, along with those of other writers of his era, are telling. They display the high level of literary development that typically occurs only in an advanced, stable culture that treasures and promotes the arts and other civilized endeavors.

Kalidasa's poetry still resonates with readers today, and he is remembered as the greatest Indian author of all time. Shown here is a depiction of the famous writer at work.

Gold in Decline

The stability of the Gupta realm was not as long-lasting as Chandragupta II may have hoped. After his death in 415, the empire began a slow but steady decline. During the reign of his son, Kumara Gupta, a fierce Asian people—the Huns—invaded western India and did widespread damage to the stability of the empire. Some of the Huns proceeded even further westward, attacked Europe, and threatened Rome.

Kumara Gupta's son, Skanda Gupta, was able to decisively defeat these intruders. Despite his victories, a new wave of Huns, the White Huns, arrived in the closing years of the fifth century, and they were not so easy to resist. The exact origins of the White Huns are unknown. Scholars know that they were called the "White" Huns because of their location within China: Hunnic tribes in the North were called "Black" Huns, "Green" or "Blue" Huns lived in the South, "Red" Huns lived in the East, and "White" Huns hailed from the West. Because of the ongoing decline of the Gupta realm, including its military, they managed to seize the Punjab and then pushed eastward into the Ganges Valley.

In a stark historical parallel, these events closely coincided with the fall of the Western Roman Empire in the 470s, also caused mainly by foreign invasions. A makeshift alliance of Indian kings was finally able to defeat the Huns around 530, but the Gupta Empire was a shell of its former self. In the decades that followed, the empire continued to crumble. Eventually, Magadha's history repeated itself, and once more, the region fragmented into many small and largely ineffectual states. Whatever dreams and ambitions the leaders of these states may have had, they and their successors faced a harsh reality: The magnificent empires that had dominated India's ancient era were gone forever.

chapter seven

EVERYDAY LIFE IN ANCIENT INDIA

D espite the many ups and downs of life in an ancient empire, daily life for Indian citizens was filled with the same kinds of things that fill peoples' daily lives today: family, entertainment, marriage, fashion, and culture. Using a variety of sources, scholars have been able to piece together ideas of what those things looked like and how they influenced society and its customs.

In some cases, these sources are archeological, such as excavated streets, houses, furniture, tools, jewelry, coins, and other artifacts. In other cases, historical documentation describes ancient Indian customs and institutions in surviving written documents, especially the *Arthashastra* and other documents from the Mauryan era. Surviving ancient sculptures, which often show clothing and jewelry styles; religious beliefs and customs; social, political,

and military practices; and much more contribute to modern understanding of ancient Indian life.

Continuity and Change

Ancient Indian society was far from static and unchanging over the course of its dozens of centuries of existence. Architectural design, home goods, family life, popular fashion, craft and artistic styles, social customs, and the institutions, rules, and laws imposed by governments evolved and changed from age to age. Of course, as in all times and places, nobles and other wealthy people had bigger, better-built homes, more belongings, finer clothes, and more social privileges and opportunities than those in the lower classes. Archaeologists are often able to determine an ancient person's social status by examining their personal belongings.

GATEWAY TO THE GARDEN

Wealthy owners of townhomes in India's Gupta period almost always included private gardens in their houses, described here by scholar Jeannine Auboyer:

> The garden was looked after with great care; it contained a vegetable garden which the mistress of the house supervised personally and in which she grew the medicinal plants needed for treating the family's [sicknesses]. The rest of the garden was decorated with spreading trees, flowering shrubs and banana-plants. The general effect was enhanced by a few ornamental pools whose sparkling surfaces were half-hidden by pink lotus blossoms ... A swing was fixed up in some shady spot, from a tree-branch or on a wooden [platform], and adults as well as children [used] it from springtime onwards.[1]

1. Jeannine Auboyer, *Daily Life in Ancient India: From Approximately 200 BC to AD 700*, Simon Watson Taylor, trans. London, UK: Asia Publishing House, 1965, p. 135.

Still, overall, life did not change dramatically over the course of India's ancient period. Changing laws and religious customs evolved through the years, but in general, there was a strong sense of tradition and continuity. If a person could have magically transported from a city in one of the Mahājanapadas in 500 BC to the Gupta capital of Pataliputra a thousand years later, they could quickly and easily have learned to fit in. A visit to the central outdoor marketplace, for instance, would have been an almost identical experience in both times and places. French scholar Jeannine Auboyer described what the traveler would be likely to see:

> Crowds of shoppers strolled along in front of the shelves piled high with green vegetables, fruits of all kinds, candied sugar, cooked rice and prepared foods ready for eating, whose pungent odours contrasted with the more delicate scents given off by the pyramids of incense sticks and sandalwood arranged on the perfumers' counters. Elsewhere, jewellers and goldsmiths cut and arranged precious stones, and polished different metals, while ... tailors cut and stitched garments; smiths hammered out copper vessels; [and] weavers worked their looms and sold materials. [Meanwhile] rich and poor, deliverymen and shoppers, hirelings and porters elbowed each other.[29]

Even today, India is famous for its busy marketplaces. Though they would have looked different in ancient times, the energy would still be recognizable.

House and Home

How these shoppers and merchants lived varied greatly depending on their financial circumstances. Just as in modern times, ancient people lived in dwellings that reflected something about their lives; whether a house was new or old, rural or urban, or large or small, it could tell a lot about its inhabitants. Throughout India's ancient centuries, poor country folk—mostly subsistence farmers and laborers—typically lived in modest, one-story huts. These were made from dried mud or thatch (tightly bundled tree branches). Such a house commonly had one or two small rooms, no more than one window, and a dirt floor, sometimes overlaid by mats made of interwoven river reeds. There was little furniture; people sat on the floor, so chairs were not necessary. However, there was often a bed, constructed out of a bamboo framework with reed mats or other, softer materials piled on top. The residents cooked their food in a crude fireplace fueled by wood and dried plants.

Such dwellings probably existed in large towns and cities, too, but their numbers, size, and features are unknown because they were made of perishable materials that have left little or no trace in the archaeological record. What has survived from these ancient cities, however, shows that many townhouses were larger and more comfortable. Their owners were middle-class workers, such as craftsmen, artisans, or merchants; or upper-class nobles,

courtiers, and rich traders who were able to pay for comfort. Members of these classes could afford houses made of wood or brick. Brick was used for residential structures mainly in the Harappan towns of the third and second millennia BC; in contrast, wood and bamboo were the principal structural materials for townhouses in the Mauryan and Gupta periods.

A typical expensive townhouse in the fourth or fifth century AD, for example, had two or three stories supported by a sturdy wooden framework. It had two entrances—one facing the street, the other opening into a private backyard containing gardens. The rooms were divided from one another not by solid walls, but by woven mats hung vertically from bamboo poles set horizontally in the ceilings.

Thus, the layout of each story could be changed relatively easily by rearranging the poles and mats. Auboyer described other aspects of construction and layout:

A veranda with columns shaded the ground floor and the others had balconies. The top storey, under the eaves, used for storing the family's valuable and reserve provisions, was lighted by gable-windows whose brightly painted wooden frames could be seen and admired from the street … The roofs themselves might be thatched, tiled or shingled. Sometimes, they were terraced instead, and the family could then come up to enjoy the coolness of the night air and watch the stars. The windows were masked by lattice-work screens, by mats or by curtains decorated with geometrical patterns; the windows were also often fitted with solid shutters ... Texts [hint at] the existence of a secret chamber, or at least a secret compartment ... the family treasure was hidden there.[30]

Such comfortable homes featured plenty of furniture, including comfortable beds, stacked with pillows and sometimes canopies above. There were benches and small sofas for sitting, as well as wooden tables on which women placed their makeup and toiletries or where members of the family played chess (which may have been invented in ancient India).

The kitchen was typically outside in the garden area. It consisted of a brick hearth for cooking and tables for preparing food, all sheltered from the sun and rain by a canopy held up by bamboo poles.

Family Ties

The average house in ancient India was home to a large family. Not much is known about family structure and customs in the Harappan and Vedic ages, but from the Mauryan era onward, extended families were common. These included not only a father, mother, and their children, but also grandparents, aunts, uncles, and servants. Furthermore, an unknown proportion of families, particularly among the upper-class Kshatriyas, practiced polygamy. The husband and father, who was the head of the household, might have two or more wives, each of whom bore him children.

By custom, the head of household had many crucial duties and roles. He had the final word on all major decisions concerning the household, such as arranging marriages for his children, though it is likely that he would consult with various relatives, including his wife. He was also the primary breadwinner and worked to earn the money needed to support the family. The man also oversaw religious worship in the home; for example, the father led the family in the performance of rituals at an in-house altar.

Within this system, the family matriarch had a lower social status and more limited freedom than her husband. On the other hand, she had almost complete authority over domestic affairs, including raising children, meal preparation, and growing herbs the family used for medicines. She was rarely allowed to leave the family compound, however; when she did, commonly to attend religious festivals or go on family outings, she was almost always accompanied by a male adult and wore a shawl over her body and a veil across her face.

Ancient Indian women were also subject to various punishments for a wide variety of infractions, some of them quite minor by modern standards. Some of these punishments, typically in the form of a beating, were at the discretion of her husband or father. There were also monetary fines (measured in *panas*) for bad behavior that were imposed by a council of community elders. According to the *Arthashastra*,

If a woman engages herself in … drinking in the face of an order to the contrary, she shall be fined three panas. She shall pay a fine of six panas for going out at daytime … she shall pay a fine of twelve panas if she goes out to see another man or for sports. For the same offences committed at night the fines shall be doubled. If a woman goes out while the husband is asleep or [drunk], or if she shuts the door of the house against her husband, she shall be fined twelve panas.[31]

For a woman in Mauryan or Gupta society, her wedding day was supposed to be one of the most significant days of her life. Wealthy women wore a beautiful dress and took part in an extravagant wedding ceremony and feast, attended by hundreds of people. Before the marriage, her father had paid her future husband a dowry, which was money or valuables to help support her in the marriage. It was common for a father to promise his daughter to a future husband when she was between the ages of 8 and 10, even if the wedding itself did not take place until later. Ages 10 to 14 were common for marriage for girls; boys were generally a little older when they wed. Because marriage was viewed as a sacred institution, divorce was rare.

To this day, Indian weddings are often large affairs that span many days and can include hundreds of guests.

THE GREAT STUPA AT SANCHI

Because religion was among the most important social institutions in ancient India, governments and communities put a great deal of time and money into erecting temples. These structures were designed to both glorify the gods and inspire awe in worshippers. The most basic form of these temples, which began to appear in the first millennium BC, was the stupa. It began as a circular earthen burial mound, but over time, people transformed stupas into dome-shaped temples constructed of fired bricks or stone blocks that were often plastered and painted.

As time went on, builders added circular walls, fences, or other enclosures around stupas, some of which became very large and elaborate. Among the more outstanding examples is the Great Stupa at Sanchi, a Buddhist temple in north-central India. Still in good condition, it is 120 feet (37 m) across and 54 feet (15.5 m) high. Hindu temples also utilized the stupa form, though often in more developed adaptations. These included the *shikhara*, a pagoda-like tower that was essentially a stupa extended upward for several stories. Hindu temples, especially from the Gupta period onward, were typically adorned, inside and out, with elaborate, sometimes crowded displays of statues and other sculptures depicting the gods and their legendary deeds.

Slavery in Ancient India

Slavery in ancient times was very different from systems of slavery in more recent times. From Mauryan times onward, a majority of middle-class and upper-class families owned slaves. People obtained slaves in several ways. Some were prisoners taken during wars fought among Indian states; others were foreigners bought by Indian merchants, who then sold them to Indian customers; and others were children born to slaves who were already part of a family. In addition, it was possible for a person to voluntarily sell themselves into slavery, on a temporary basis, as a way of settling a debt. Settling a debt this way was dangerous, however, as someone who committed a criminal act after serving as a slave would be enslaved for life.

Evidence suggests that life for most ancient Indian slaves was hard—but not always unbearable or hopeless. Though they did have to do difficult physical labor, such as carrying the family water from a stream, fountain, or other water source to the house, many of their duties were similar to everyday service—for example, helping the lady of the household clean, prepare meals, and garden. Still, slaves could be beaten for breaking rules or laziness, though laws often limited the severity of punishments. Moreover, Mauryan law actually imposed fines, some of them heavy, on owners who mistreated their slaves.

Interestingly, Indian slaves had the right to earn money. With their master's permission, a slave could do work outside the home and be paid for it. Moreover, the slave could save up this money and, if the master was willing, buy their freedom. Some masters allowed their female slaves to marry free men and live at home with them; the condition was that such women had to return to the master's house each day and perform certain chores.

Law and Order

Everyday life in the Mauryan and Gupta eras was just as shaped by new bureaucracy as it was by traditional social, religious, and economic institutions, including faith, marriage, and work. Governmental administration, law, and structure affected people of all social classes and castes. For instance, just as people in nearly every modern nation must pay taxes on a routine basis, ancient Indians owed a percentage of their earnings and production to the government. In fact, the Mauryans' huge administrative bureaucracies and armies could not have been maintained without large-scale tax collection, and as such, the office of revenue and taxation was one of the biggest departments of the Mauryan government. This office employed thousands of officials, tax collectors, and clerks working in every corner of the empire and all reporting back to a central authority.

Among the most lucrative taxes were tolls levied on all manner of trade goods—from food and drink to clothing, crafted items, building materials, and more. Toll collectors set up booths at all town and city gates so they could inspect every person and pack animal seeking entry. This system was devised by Kautilya in his *Arthashastra*. "When merchants with their merchandise arrive at the toll-gate," Kautilya wrote,

four or five collectors shall take down who the merchants are, whence they come, what amount of merchandise they have brought ... Those whose merchandise has not been stamped with sealmark shall pay twice the amount of toll. For counterfeit seal they shall pay eight times the toll ... Imported commodities shall pay 1/5th of their value as toll.

Of flower, fruit, vegetables (sáka), roots (múla), bulbous roots (kanda) ... seeds, dried fish, and dried meat, the superintendent shall receive 1/6th as toll ... Of cloths (vastra), quadrupeds, bipeds, threads, cotton, scents, medicines, wood, bamboo, fibres (valkala), skins, and clay-pots; of grains, oils, sugar (kshára), salt, liquor (madya) cooked rice and the like, he shall receive 1/20th or 1/25th as toll.[32]

CULINARY CULTURE

Ancient Indians consumed a wide range of nutritious foods. As with most things, not much is known about the eating habits of the Harappans and early Vedic people. Some evidence shows that they grew barley, wheat, rice, peas, melons, and dates. For protein, they fished and raised sheep, pigs, and cattle. After the spread of Buddhism and Jainism, both of which discouraged the killing of animals, meat-eating became much less common. Some people, particularly among the Kshatriya caste, still ate meat but never from animals that give milk; birds, including chicken, and fish, however, were acceptable.

By the Gupta era, most Indians were vegetarians. Rice was a mainstay of the diet, including thick soups made of rice and vegetables and rice flour, which people used to make bread-pancakes (*chapati*) that are still widely popular in India today. Other important food staples included barley, wheat, beans (which were both boiled and fried), many varieties of vegetables and fruits, and honey and sugar cane for sweeteners. The most common drinks were water and milk, but many adults also drank alcoholic beverages made by fermenting coconuts, rice, or barley.

Chapati *is still a popular dish today.*

This system provided a win-win situation for the government: They received money whether or not merchants agreed to pay the toll. In fact, noncompliance with the law could net the government a higher profit than they were able to get from law-abiding citizens.

Of course, governments rarely want to encourage lawlessness, and the ancient empires were no different. Despite their largely humane approach to rule, the Mauryan kings, including Aśoka, maintained a large network of spies. While these intelligence agents had several tasks, one of their primary tasks was to make sure that nobody was cheating on their taxes. They also performed the difficult and dangerous work of keeping an eye on enemy nations and agents.

The government also maintained numerous constructive policies that promoted the welfare of the citizens and even local wildlife. There were plans in place for avoiding large numbers of casualties and alleviating suffering during national disasters, for example. Edicts with the force of law instructed people on what to do in case of floods, fires, disease epidemics, famine, rat infestations, and so forth. Strong kings pledged to feed their citizens during famines and other catastrophes.

In addition, the same rulers maintained public lands that combined the modern concepts of game preserve and national forest. The Mauryan kings, for instance, were deeply concerned about certain kinds of wildlife preservation, especially with regard to elephants. They set aside nature preserves, where government agents would make sure that no poachers were killing elephants or other creatures illegally. Such modern policies—that would not be out of place in a nation today—are among the factors that ranked India's Mauryan and Gupta societies among the most advanced and enlightened in the ancient world.

THE LEGACY OF ANCIENT INDIA

More than almost any other region, the legacies of India's ancient civilizations still echo today. Over the course of the region's development and the rises and falls of its many empires, military heroes, and religious pioneers, a large and rich collection of remarkably modern cultural and religious ideas developed. Some of these ideas remained relevant and impactful in later dynasties and are still resonant today. The Hindu faith is a clear example: It is a tradition that began as far back as the Vedic Age and to this day is one of the world's leading religions. Modern India may not be much like its ancient predecessors politically or socially, but it is a testament to ancient social, political, and religious philosophies that so many ideas that emerged during those eras are still valued today.

The Arrival of Islam
In all the centuries following the demise of the Gupta Empire, India never ceased to be a huge, diverse region with expansive human and material resources. As in the past, this quality made it enormously attractive to outsiders who hoped to harness and exploit those resources. The first major, post-Gupta foreign incursion was a series of invasions by various Muslim groups. Many of these invasions were successful because, in the wake of the Gupta Empire, India was primarily made up of small, relatively weak kingdoms, few of which had any sense of unity or allied relationships.

The initial Muslim intrusion in the 600s was little more than a large-scale raid that had no lasting effect on Indian culture—but there was more to come. A larger movement in the period of 1001 to 1027 created a Muslim base in the Punjab Plain. Furthermore, a still larger thrust that began in the late 1100s succeeded in setting up a large Muslim state in northern India. Called the Delhi Sultanate, it lasted from 1206 to 1526

The Taj Mahal is one of India's most famous tourist destinations.

and featured several dynamic dynasties of rulers. Meanwhile, soon after 1400, a number of other Islamic rulers established kingdoms in northern India. All of these early Muslim-ruled Indian states eventually fell to a new wave of invaders: the Timurids (Sunni Muslims of Asian-Mongol descent). In 1526, the leader of the Timurids, Babur (Arabic for "tiger"), established the Mughal dynasty and empire. The Mughals managed to gain control of most of northern India by about 1600, during the reign of Babur's grandson, Akbar.

With a few exceptions, the Mughals, especially Akbar, were tolerant of Hinduism, which continued to be practiced by a majority of Indians. Like the Kushans before them, these rulers did not want to impose strictly Muslim artistic styles on the country; rather, they respected and promoted a wide range of styles.

The famous Taj Mahal, in Agra (in northern India), is a prominent example. Built by the Mughal emperor Shah Jahān as a mausoleum for his beloved wife, it was completed in 1648, while the outlying buildings were completed in 1653. This splendid structure is illustrative of the cultural fusion that occurred in the Mughal Age because it combines elements of Persian, Indian, Islamic, and other architectural styles.

Colonization Under British Rule

In the early 1700s, the Mughal Empire began to decline. This was in part because a number of smaller states arose in various parts of the subcontinent and challenged Mughal power. Chief among these rivals was the Maratha Confederacy, centered in its capital of Pune in southwestern India. During this period of infighting among Indian states, another foreign power—Britain—was beginning to branch out into the subcontinent. The British colonization of India began with trade; after securing permission from the Mughal rulers, the British East India Company set up trading posts in India in the 1600s.

As the company's economic base steadily expanded, so did its power. It began using hired soldiers—a mix of Europeans and native Indians (called sepoys)—to enforce its will. The company took over the Bengal region in the 1750s and 1760s and thereafter continued to expand its influence, largely at the expense of the Mughals, Marathas, and other native Indians. Rising discontent among Indians over the company's expanding power, coupled with the continued decline of Mughal power, led to the Indian Mutiny (or Sepoy Mutiny) of 1857. Although the native rebels fought courageously, the company's forces, reinforced by thousands of regular British troops, crushed them.

The British government in London now saw that the East India Company had accumulated far too much power in the region. It promptly abolished the company and instituted direct British control over most of the subcontinent; British rule in India subsequently became known as the British Raj beginning in 1858. Among Britain's many colonies around the world at the time, India was by far its most productive and financially lucrative. In the years to come, the British would be extremely reluctant to part with the region, which they came to call the jewel in Britain's colonial crown.

No matter how economically valuable India was to Britain, the right of self-rule was even more valuable to Indians. In 1885, not long after the establishment of the Raj, several prominent Indians formed the Indian National Congress. Its goal was to work toward establishing independence from the British. At first, what became known as the Indian independence movement made little progress. However, this began to change shortly before 1920 with the emergence of a brilliant and courageous Indian political activist named Mohandas Gandhi. He advocated a strategy of relentless nonviolent protests, many of which he personally led, along with the boycotting of British goods.

The struggle took many years and was not free of bloodshed—but the approach worked. In 1946, the British agreed to grant India its independence the following year. However, by this time, members of the large Muslim

The British East India Company established trade relations with India and quickly grew in power.

minority worried that the Hindu majority would suppress their rights in the new country. Muslim leaders called for the partition, or division, of India into two new countries: one ruled by Muslims, the other by Hindus. Thus, in August 1947, the two nations—Pakistan and the Republic of India—were established. At first, Muslim Pakistan was divided into two sections—West Pakistan, centered in the Indus Valley, and East Pakistan, situated north of the Bay of Bengal. In 1971, East Pakistan forcibly broke away and became the independent nation of Bangladesh.

The World's Most Populous Democracy

In the years since gaining independence, India has become one of the world's most influential and diverse nations. In fact, the country is so diverse that they have no single national language; instead, there are 22. This is hardly surprising, as it would be difficult to choose just 1 from the more than 1,721 languages spoken throughout the region. In fact, the Census of India of 2001 listed 122 "major languages," which are languages spoken by more than 10,000 people.

India officially became independent in 1947. Indian National Cadet Corps students are shown here celebrating India's Independence Day.

Though India is a relatively new democracy, it is the most populous, and the civic duty tied to that distinction is something that Indians clearly take seriously—in the 2014 general election, turnout hovered around 60 percent. The United States, by comparison, typically has around 59 percent of eligible voters cast ballots. Additionally, India has emerged as the fastest growing major economy, aided by an increasing focus on banking, technology, and structural reform, with projects designed to increase the amount of goods made in India and to increase Wi-Fi access at popular tourist locations.

Despite the modern flourishes that India is experiencing as a country, its inhabitants have never given up their ties to a long past that is rich with history. Indians keep in close contact with the ancient cultural, linguistic, religious, and artistic features that made the subcontinent one of the most unique regions in world history. In fact, many have argued that it is precisely because of this powerful connection to a strong foundation that India today is on the front lines of the charge into the future.

Notes

Introduction:
Facts and Figures

1. Quoted in Bob Sipchen, "A Vivid Portrait of India's Religious, Cultural Riches," *Los Angeles Times*, June 27, 1999. articles.latimes.com/1999/jun/27/travel/tr-50520.

2. Alain Daniélou, *A Brief History of India*. New York, NY: Simon and Schuster, 2003, PDF e-book.

Chapter One:
Early Empires

3. Bridget Allchin and Raymond Allchin, *The Rise of Civilization in India and Pakistan*. Cambridge, UK: Cambridge University Press, 1982, p. 171.

4. John Keay, *India: A History*. New York, NY: Grove Press, 2010, PDF e-book.

Chapter Two:
Conquering Heroes?

5. Quoted in David N. Lorenzen, "Religion, Skin Colour and Language: Ārya and Non-Ārya in the Vedic Period," in *Who Invented Hinduism: Essays on Religion in History*. New Delhi, India: Yoda Press, 2006, p. 165.

6. B.B. Lal, "Why Perpetuate Myths? A Fresh Look at Indian History," International Forum for India's Heritage, accessed July 11, 2017. www.ifih.org/whyperpetuatemyths.html.

7. Quoted in Lal, "Why Perpetuate Myths?."

8. Keay, *India*, PDF e-book.

9. Quoted in Keay, *India*, PDF e-book.

10. Lal, "Why Perpetuate Myths?."

11. David Frawley, "The Myth of the Aryan Invasion of India," Knowledge of Reality, accessed July 12, 2017. www.sol.com.au/kor/16_01.htm.

12. Keay, *India*, PDF e-book.

Chapter Three:
East Meets West

13. Keay, *India*, PDF e-book.

14. Quoted in Stephen Bost, Ancient History, *Ancient Warriors and Stories of Courage*. San Jose, CA: Writers Club Press, 2002, p. 114.

15. Arrian, *The Campaigns of Alexander*. New York, NY: Penguin, 2003, PDF e-book.

Chapter Four:
The Rise of Magadha

16. Quintus Curtius Rufus, *The History of Alexander*, John Yardley, trans. New York, NY: Penguin, 2005, PDF e-book.

17. Keay, *India*, PDF e-book.

18. Kautilya, "Indian History Sourcebook: Kautilya: From *The Arthashastra*, c. 250 BCE," R. Shamasastry, trans. Indian History Sourcebook, accessed July 13, 2017. sourcebooks.fordham.edu/india/kautilya1.asp#Book%20 I,%20Chapter%2019.

19. Quoted in Radha Kumud Mookerji, *Chandragupta Maurya and His Times*. Delhi, India: Motilal Banarsidass, 1966, p. 58.

20. Vincent Arthur Smith, *The Oxford History of India: From the Earliest Times to the End of 1911*. Oxford, UK: Oxford University Press, 1920, p. 75.

21. Aśoka, "The Edicts of King Asoka," Ven S. Dhammika, trans., The Edicts of King Ashoka, accessed July 13, 2017. www.cs.colostate.edu/~malaiya/ ashoka.html..

22. Keay, *India*, PDF e-book.

Chapter Five:
Gods and Men

23. Ralph T.H. Griffith, trans., "Hymn XXV. Varuṇa," Sacred Texts, accessed July 13, 2017. www.sacred-texts.com/hin/rigveda/rv01025.htm.

Chapter Six:
The Golden Age of Guptas

24. Keay, *India*, PDF e-book.

25. Keay, *India*, PDF e-book.

26. Faxian, *A Record of Buddhistic Kingdoms*, James Legge, trans. Oxford, UK: Clarendon Press, 1886, p. 79.

27. Faxian, *A Record of Buddhistic Kingdoms*, p. 79.

28. Kalidasa, "The Birth of the War-God," Sacred Texts, accessed July 14, 2017. www.sacred-texts.com/hin/sha/sha16.htm.

Chapter Seven:
Everyday Life in Ancient India

29. Jeannine Auboyer, *Daily Life in Ancient India: From Approximately 200 BC to AD 700*, Simon Watson Taylor, trans. London, UK: Asia Publishing House, 1965, pp. 121–122.

30. Auboyer, *Daily Life in Ancient India*, p. 133.

31. Kautilya, "Indian History Sourcebook: Kautilya: From the *Arthashastra*, c. 250 BCE: On Gender Issues," R. Shamasastry, trans., Indian History Sourcebook, accessed July 14, 2017. sourcebooks.fordham.edu/india/kautilya2.asp.

32. Kautilya, "Kautilya's *Arthashastra*: Book II, 'The Duties of Government Superintendents,'" accessed July 14, 2017. www.columbia.edu/itc/mealac/pritchett/00litlinks/kautilya/book02.htm.

For More Information

Books

Chakrabarti, Dilip K. *The Battle for Ancient India: An Essay in the Sociopolitics of Indian Archaeology*. New Delhi, India: Aryan Books International, 2008.
For as long as there have been archeologists studying ancient India, there have been fierce debates about what the evidence actually says; this book offers insights into leading theories.

Goldman, Robert P., Sally Sutherland Goldman, and Barend A. Van Nooten, eds. *The Ramayana of Valmiki: An Epic of Ancient India; Yuddhakanda*. Princeton, NJ: Princeton University Press, 2016.
The *Ramayana* is an ancient epic poem that tells the story of the divine prince Rama, and it is one of the most important pieces of world literature.

Lahiri, Nayanjot. *Ashoka in Ancient India*. Cambridge, MA: Harvard University Press, 2015.
Read about the legendary king Aśoka in this biography that seeks to determine what parts of his legend are fact and which are fiction.

Sharma, Ram S. *India's Ancient Past*. Delhi, India: Oxford University Press, 2005.
This book covers a wide array of ancient Indian civilizations and charts the cultural, linguistic, religious, and geopolitical changes that spanned the centuries.

Singh, Girish P. *Republics, Kingdoms, Towns and Cities in Ancient India*. New Delhi, India: D.K. Printworld, 2003.
This book focuses on how ancient peoples built and planned the places in which they lived.

Verma, S. K. *Political History of Ancient India*. Delhi, India: Manglam Publications, 2010.
Verma examines the political institutions of ancient India's leaders—from the Vedic age to the Mauryan dynasty and beyond.

Websites

Ancient India
(www.ancientindia.co.uk)
   This website, run by the British Museum, explores the geographical, religious, archeological, and artistic development of ancient Indian civilizations.

Buddhism
(www.bbc.co.uk/religion/religions/buddhism)
   Provided by the BBC, this useful website provides links explaining many aspects of one of the world's most popular faiths.

Jainism
(www.bbc.co.uk/religion/religions/jainism/)
   This informative BBC-hosted website offers many links to articles and details about the important ancient Indian religion of Jainism.

The Library at A Handful of Leaves
(www.ahandfulofleaves.org/Library.html)
   A Handful of Leaves provides readers with extensive resources for further reading on Buddhism, ancient Indian civilizations, and language.

The Story of India
(www.pbs.org/thestoryofindia)
   This six-part collaboration between PBS and the BBC takes readers through a detailed history of ancient India: its cultures, religion, food, and political struggle from 60,000 BC to 2009.

Index

Picture Credits

Cover Godong/robertharding/Getty Images; pp. 6–7 (background) nevskyphoto/iStock/Thinkstock; p. 6 (top-left) suronin/Shutterstock.com; p. 6 (top-right) pzAxe/Shutterstock.com; p. 6 (bottom-left) Rogers Fund and Purchase, Joseph Pulitzer Bequest, by exchange, 1957/Metropolitan Museum of Art; p. 6 (bottom-right) Purchase, Mr. and Mrs. Peter Findlay Gift, 1979/ Metropolitan Museum of Art; pp. 7 (top-left), 70 Samuel Eilenberg Collection, Gift of Samuel Eilenberg, 1987/Metropolitan Museum of Art; p. 7 (top-right) Ann Ronan Pictures/Print Collector/Getty Images; p. 7 (bottom-left) Anonymous Gift, 1978/Metropolitan Museum of Art; p. 7 (bottom-middle) Purchase, Florence and Herbert Irving Gift, 1991/Metropolitan Museum of Art; p. 7 (bottom-right) courtesy of the Library of Congress; p. 9 (top) Boris Stroujko/ Shutterstock.com; p. 9 (bottom) Don Mammoser/Shutterstock.com; pp. 10–11 Natalia Deriabina/Shutterstock.com; p. 12 Natalia Davidovich/Shutterstock.com; p. 13 Jorisvo/iStock/Thinkstock; pp. 16–17 SAM PANTHAKY/AFP/Getty Images; p. 18 Nadeem Khawar/Moment Open/Getty Images; p. 21 courtesy of the Museum of Fine Arts, Boston; p. 22 Jiri Vaclavek/Shutterstock.com; p. 23 Marben/Shutterstock.com; p. 28 Education Images/UIG via Getty Images; p. 31 Robert Harding/robertharding/Getty Images; p. 34 Culture Club/Getty Images; p. 38 Godong/Universal Images Group via Getty Images; p. 40 Gift of Alexander Smith Cochran, 1913/Metropolitan Museum of Art; pp. 42–43, 50, 72 courtesy of the Los Angeles County Museum of Art; p. 48 Rainer Lesniewski/ Shutterstock.com; p. 53 Wienerbund/Wikimedia Commons; p. 56 Lileephoto/ Shutterstock.com; p. 60 Claudine Van Massenhove/Shutterstock.com; pp. 62–63 Mary Griggs Burke Collection, Gift of the Mary and Jackson Burke Foundation, 2015/Metropolitan Museum of Art; pp. 66–67 Rogers Fund, 1955/Metropolitan Museum of Art; p. 76 Kalidasa indinting the 'Cloud Messenger' 375 AD (litho), Almond, William Douglas (1866–1916)/Private Collection/Bridgeman Images; p. 80 Radiokafka/Shutterstock.com; p. 83 Milind Arvind Ketkar/Shutterstock.com; p. 86 norikko/Shutterstock.com; p. 89 Rich Jones Photography/Moment/Getty Images; p. 91 Tethys Imaging LLC/Shutterstock.com; p. 92 NOAH SEELAM/ AFP/Getty Images.

About the Author

Cecilia Jennings first became interested in the ancient world when she learned about Cleopatra in her fourth grade social studies class, and she never looked back. She is particularly interested in the spread of religious ideas and practices across regions and time. She lives in Wisconsin and works part-time as a cheese monger, but despite tasting lots of fancy cheeses, her favorite is still pepper jack.